SMACHT

THE DISCIPLINE OF SUCCESS

Stories, Insights & Questions to Drive
Your Business & Personal Success

PÁDRAIC Ó MÁILLE

OAK·TREE·PRESS

Published by Oak Tree Press, Cork T12 XY2N, Ireland.
www.oaktreepress.com / www.SuccessStore.com

© 2024 Pádraic Ó Máille.

Cover image: nexus plexus / 123rf.com

Cover design: Kieran O'Connor Design.

A catalogue record for this book is available from the British Library.

ISBN 978-1-78119-624-3 Paperback
ISBN 978-1-78119-625-0 PDF
ISBN 978-1-78119-626-7 ePub
ISBN 978-1-78119-627-4 Kindle

CONTENTS

ATTITUDE

CASH

HUMAN BEINGS

TIME

DEDICATION

For my wife, Annie: Once upon a time, I met a girl in The Lenaboy Arms and that story transformed everything, and continues to do so. Thank you when needed for seeing through me but always for seeing me through. Long may we continue to share great stories together.

For my children, Shane, Sarah, Harry and Óige: You may not always have listened to my stories, or laughed in the right places, but when I look at you I can say proudly we've done some things right.

For my grandchildren, Zara and Finn: May you always carry a great story with you wherever you go, because storytellers rule the world.

For my dogs, Mac, Eager and Potter: You have lived through every story with me for the past 40 years, including the many sitting ducks I missed along the way. But irrespective of the outcome, you always wagged your tails and radiated unconditional love. May you continue to bring the game home 'oven-ready' as you did so many times in the past.

For my customers: Thank you for providing me with the purpose for getting up enthusiastically each morning and inspiring me to create. May our outcomes together continue to bring you purpose, prosperity and peace.

For my teachers: Your influence is incalculable and you'll never know for sure quite where it ends. May you continue to educate and inspire and transform. This book is littered with great teacher stories.

And finally, to my creditors: Thank you for keeping me inspired and on my toes.

FOREWORD

Pádraic Ó Máille has been a good friend of mine for over 30 years. He creates positive energy in everyone fortunate enough to spend time with him.

The first time I saw Pádraic in action was when I asked him to give a workshop to our team at *Foinse*, an Irish language newspaper we were producing from Carraroe in County Galway. His ability to actively engage with us in terms of creating our vision, strategy and actions formed the foundation for *Foinse* becoming the most-read Irish language newspaper in the country up to that time.

Pádraic has supported and mentored both sports people and business people for many years, helping them on their journeys to success.

He has an energetic, active and engaging style of storytelling, questioning and challenging. This creates space for individual and team reflection, resulting in deep personal learning and clear actions to help you bring your game to the next level.

Pádraic calls the process SMACHT, based on the Irish word for discipline, which is fundamental to success.

I wish Pádraic continued success in making a significant difference to people's lives and businesses and I wish you, the reader, enjoyment and valuable lessons from reading this book.

Pádraig Ó Céidigh
EY Entrepreneur of the Year 2002

INTRODUCTION:
HIDE THE PILL IN THE PEANUT BUTTER

We must all suffer from one of two pains:
the pain of discipline or the pain of regret.
The difference is discipline weighs ounces,
while regret weighs tons.

Jim Rohn

For all of his gruff exterior, Reilly is an out-and-out softie when it comes to dogs. When his Labrador, Potter, emerged from the frozen lake like a drowned rat, Reilly noticed there was something wrong with the dog's tail.

As the day wore on, it seemed the pain intensified as the dog's moans escalated from whimpering to barking to shrieking.

Reilly called his old buddy, Séamus McManus, an iconic Galway vet, and explained the situation.

Having listened attentively to the facts, Seamus diagnosed that it was most likely a case of 'limber tail syndrome', a condition that Labradors are prone to, but one that would heal up quickly.

In the short term, however, it might help to give him a buffered aspirin – not paracetamol – to ease the pain and reduce the inflammation.

Reilly procured the tablets and proceeded to give the dog the pill. But try as he might, that dog refused to swallow the pill.

Reilly pushed it down his mouth, shoved it back his throat, and held his mouth closed but every time Potter would squirm out of his clutch and spit the pill out.

In desperation, Reilly called Séamus back and explained his quandary.

Séamus is a man of few words and calmly replied, "Hide the pill in peanut butter".

"What?", said Reilly.

"Hide the pill in peanut butter."

You'd want to have seen that dog's first experience of peanut butter.

First he sniffed it. Then he licked it. And as large globules of drool fell from his jaws, he proceeded to scoff the entire lot, pill and all.

It took about 20 minutes for the moaning to subside. Then the dog turned on his back and commenced to snore loudly and sonorously.

INSIGHTS

- That's the thing about pills. They can reduce pain, solve problems and virtually save your life. But in their raw state, they can be hard to swallow.

- Your ideas and communications are exactly like the pill in the story above. Your messages can solve great problems for your audience but, first, you've got to get them to swallow the pill. In order to do that, it will help greatly to 'hide the pill in peanut butter'.

- The single most powerful, effective and impactful way to make your ideas and messages stick is to present them in story format.
- Think of the last presentation you attended. The chances are it was a PowerPoint presentation, loaded with facts; 90% of all business presentations are fact-based.
- The problem with facts are that they're hard to swallow and digest.

THE PILL IN THIS BOOK

On 8 February 2011, bang smack in the middle of the worst economic recession business-owners had ever experienced, Reilly was facilitating a tense meeting in the hallowed Board Room of the Golf Club in Adare Manor, County Limerick.

Gathered around were 12 business owners who were absolutely terrified at their prospects of surviving in business.

For all his idiosyncrasies, Reilly was a skilled facilitator. He dived straight into the first of three questions he had built his consulting career upon:

"What are you worried about?"

The answers didn't make for pretty listening.

Successful and proactive business people had seen their fortunes destroyed by falling sales, bad debts and negative equity.

"What can you do about it?"

The response was almost unanimous. Extreme discipline would be needed to survive: the discipline to make extra sales calls each day; to wage a relentless war on costs; and to have uncomfortable conversations with customers, employees and suppliers alike.

"What will you do about it?"

It was here that big Paulie O'Connell from Crecora Mills – not the rugby player, but equally as big, competitive and successful – threw a spanner in the proverbial works.

"There's one fundamental problem with all this discipline caper, Reilly."

"What's the problem, Paulie?", said Reilly tetchily.

"The problem, Reilly, is that I love the concept of 'discipline'. It's just that I hate the word 'discipline'."

There was widespread approval for Paulie's argument.

Reilly feared losing the dressing room and might well have, but for another intercession from Paulie.

"Reilly, you were always a great man for the Irish. What's the Irish word for 'discipline'?"

"Paulie, the Irish word for discipline is *smacht* and there's an ancient Irish proverb that proclaims: *Ní bhíonn an rath, ach mara mbíonn an smacht* (There's no success without discipline)."

The group loved the word 'smacht' (pronounced *smokt*, where the 'k' is a soft throaty sound like the '*ch*' in *loch*) and, out of sheer desperation, a mindset was agreed.

SUCCESS IS A FEW SIMPLE DISCIPLINES PRACTICED DAILY.

Over the following years, hundreds of business owners would participate in SMACHT Mastermind Groups throughout Ireland.

Almost all of them survived the recession. Many of them would go on to become super-successful and legends in their communities and industries.

What began first as a word and a mindset went on to become an operating system and a body of stories designed to make the understanding and application of those disciplines more palatable.

This book shares 52 'pills' or simple disciplines, all presented as stories, that will help drive your business and personal success.

The six simple disciplines that developed into the Smacht Operating System are contained in the SMACHT acronym:

- **Strategy:** The discipline of conscious choice and focus.
- **Marketing:** The discipline of attracting and retaining customers.
- **Attitude:** The discipline of living the best version of yourself.
- **Cash:** The discipline of becoming financially free.
- **Human Beings:** The discipline of attracting and retaining great people.
- **Time:** The discipline of living life to the full.

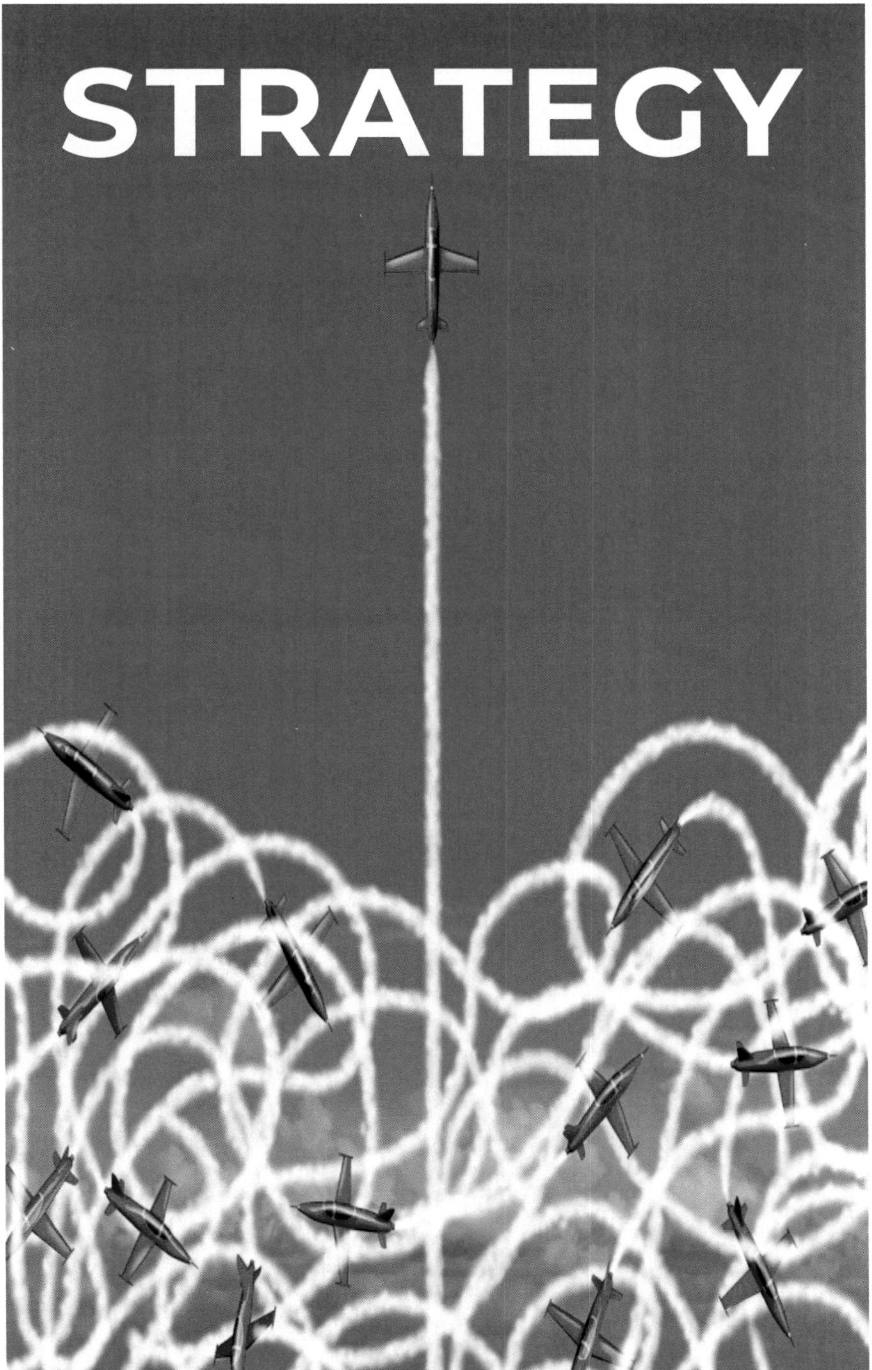
STRATEGY

1

TAKE THE RIGHT DIRECTION

If the ladder is not leaning against the right wall,
every step we take just gets us to the wrong place faster.

Stephen Covey

Reilly took his grandson, Finn, out the Flaggy Shore to show him the first of the year's Gentian Violets. They were so engrossed with the rare flowers that they didn't hear the car behind them until it honked its horn harshly.

Turning around, they saw a portly man in a big car with the passenger window down.

"How far is it to Linnane's Lobster Bar?", he shouted gruffly.

Before Reilly could get a word out, Finn piped up: "It's 24,885 miles".

The visitor was clearly unimpressed and let Finn know that in no uncertain terms: "Hey Buster, back where I come from, children are seen and not heard."

With that, he put the boot down and tore off at speed out west along the Flaggy Shore.

"That was a bit of a porky you told there, Finn", said Reilly gently.

"Not at all, Reilly. If he continues in that direction, that's exactly how far it is. The thing is, if he turned around, it's less than a mile."

Out of the mouths of babes.

INSIGHTS

- Direction in business and life is everything.
- There's no point going faster if you're going in the wrong direction.
- Be nice to people. Genuinely nice people finish on top.

QUESTIONS

- Where are you in your business now?
- Is it where you want to be?
- What are you going to do about it?

2

MODEL YOUR BUSINESS
LIKE AN AIRPLANE

When you build your business like an airplane,
it will fly far and fast.

Donald Miller, Storybrand

When everything seems to be going against you,
remember that planes take off against the wind – not with it.

Henry Ford

Reilly was sitting beside Pádraig Ó Céidigh on the 5pm Friday afternoon Aer Arann flight from Dublin to Galway. It isn't every day you get to sit beside the owner of an airline, or the current EY Entrepreneur of the Year.

Reilly had been going through a ropey patch in his business at the time and he came straight out with it to Pádraig: "Pádraig, my business seems to be stuck in a rut at the moment. How would you go about growing a business?"

Pádraig, a maths and commerce teacher before becoming a businessman, inhaled deeply and observed the plane that was preparing for take-off.

"Reilly, if you model your business on an airplane, it will fly safely and speedily and successfully. There are seven components that every successful business has in common with a plane.

"We've a few minutes before take-off. Come with me for a moment."

Pádraig proceeded to walk through the plane, introducing himself to the passengers and asking them where they were going.

Some were going home to visit sick relations. Others were going to funerals. More again were going on holidays and one American guy was going to Lisdoonvarna in search of a 'red-haired Mary'.

As they took their seats, Pádraig asks Reilly: "What do all those passengers have in common?"

"They all have an Aer Arann ticket for one thing", says Reilly smartly. "You're in the airline business, after all, and you're doing pretty good at it, judging from the full occupancy."

"You missed the point, Reilly.

"We're *not* in the airline business. Neither do we sell airline tickets.

"We're in the destination business and we sell destinations.

'The one thing every one of these passengers has is a destination – and our business is to get them there safely, speedily and successfully.

"That's the first foundation of a successful business and a successful flight: know where your customers want to go, and where you are taking them.

"Look out the window there, Reilly, and tell me what you see."

"Wings, Pádraig. Two massive big wings."

"That's the second component of growing a business and getting it airborne. The wings of a plane represent your products or services. Without products or services, you don't have a business because you have nothing to sell. You have no lift. It's the wings, or your products and services, that gives a plane and a business 'lift' and gets it airborne."

As he was speaking, there was a huge surge of noise and power and explosive movement underneath as the aircraft prepared for take-off.

"What you're experiencing now, Reilly, is what we in the aviation business call 'thrust'.

'In business, your marketing and sales are the thrust that drives your business forward and helps you arrive at your destination. Without thrust, your business is going nowhere.

"You can have the best wings or products in the world but it won't take off without thrust or effective marketing."

At precisely this moment, Eoin Kelly, the pilot, emerged from the cockpit and recognised Reilly.

"You're a long way from New Quay, Reilly", says Kelly, amiably.

"I am", says Reilly, nervously. "And if I am itself, shouldn't you be inside driving the plane not yacking out here as if you'd be drinking pints at the bar in Linnane's?"

"That's why we have co-pilots, and global positioning satellite technology, to ensure we stick to our flight plan. That frees us up to look after the needs of important passengers like you."

"The cockpit, and what it contains, is the most critical area of the plane or the business model". says Pádraig. "There are three components to a successful cockpit, which represents the leadership of your business.

"Despite all the advances of modern technology, there's no substitute for strong leadership.

"Secondly, no pilot would ever countenance taking-off without a flight plan. Yet you'd be amazed at the number of businesses that operate without a business plan!

"Thirdly, with the help of the GPS, the pilot knows at any given moment, and can track, the exact details of a number of key performance indicators such as destination, current position, altitude, wind direction, and fuel. Every business also needs to identify a core number of KPIs and track them constantly.

"Look beneath the floor there, Reilly, and tell me what you see?"

"I see big tanks, Pádraig. I guess they're the fuel tanks for carrying the petrol."

"Spot on, Reilly. Like planes need aviation fuel to operate, so also businesses need working capital to get airborne and arrive safely at their destination.

"So, Reilly, those seven simple components of an aircraft and of a business are the fundamentals of getting your business airborne and to your destination."

Reilly was so intrigued with Pádraig's masterclass that he scarcely noticed the time flying.

"This is Captain Eoin Kelly, your pilot, speaking. We will shortly be commencing our final descent into Galway Airport from a south-westerly direction over Galway Bay, passing over New Quay, Kinvara, Kilcolgan and Oranmore."

Such was the clarity of the evening sun that, as the plane banked, Reilly could clearly look in through the back window of Linnane's pub - and could actually see his stool at the bar.

That was his destination and that's where he wanted to go.

INSIGHTS

Getting a business airborne is relatively simple. Like in aviation, you need seven basic components:

- A destination to take your customers to;
- A great product or service;
- Impactful marketing;
- Strong leadership;
- A flight plan indicating your business destination, milestones along the way, and your current position;
- An accountability system to track your KPIs;
- And enough money to get you to your destination.

QUESTIONS

- Where (destination) are you taking your customers to?
- How strong are your products or services?
- How effective is your marketing and sales?
- How powerful are you as a leader?

- Have you a 'flight plan' for your business?
- Who is your accountability partner that helps you track your KPIs?
- Have you enough money to fund your business?

3

"OH, MY DARLING NORA"

Show me any person, of ordinary ability,
who will enthusiastically tell their story to four or five people
a day, and I'll show you a successful person.

Frank Bettger, *How I Raised Myself from Failure to Success in Selling*

Everyone wondered how Reilly always managed to secure tickets to all the soccer internationals. And seated in the corporate box too, surrounded by all the alickadoos and WAGs.

Nobody knew until now.

Part of Jack Charlton's remuneration package, if he succeeded in getting Ireland to its very first World Cup finals, was to provide him for an entire week with a ghillie who knew Lough Corrib.

Reilly got the job hands down. Everyone knew he was the most successful dapper on the Corrib by a country mile.

As luck would have it, conditions were ideal that May. A force four south-westerly wind ensured there was a bit of nature in the air and the choppy wave would prevent the trout getting too good a view of the bait.

The trout were taking in profusion and it wasn't long before Reilly had six fine trout colouring the deck of the boat.

This contravened the first rule of ghillieing – never upstage the client.

And it was this rule that Reilly struggled most with in life. He was a born competitor; he loved to win, and struggled to let others better him.

The problem was his client, who was equally competitive and not enjoying the best of *bonne chance*. He was either striking too quick or too slow and his humour was accordingly in decline.

Reilly sensed the *frisson* and feared the worst.

"Reilly", huffed Jack, confronting the brutal facts head-on. "We're both using the exact same lure (two fresh mayfly impaled on a size 5 copper hook). We're sat in the exact same boat. We've each have had 10 rises of a trout to our fly. You've struck on 10 occasions, landing six, and I've failed on every single occasion to even strike a ruddy fish. So Reilly, it seems to me you know something I don't know, and if you don't spill it to me you'll be swimming home."

Reilly knew his goose was cooked and uttered a silent prayer for the repose of the soul of his Uncle Stiofáin, who had shared the formula with him many years ago, vowing him to angling *omertà*.

"Jack, what's your wife's first name?", asked Reilly coyly.

"What's my wife's name got to do with ruddy fishing?", hissed Jack narkily.

"Jack, if you want to catch fish like me, you have to tell me your wife's first name."

"My wife is called Pat", says Jack uneasily.

"That won't do", says Reilly. "It's too short. Where does the name Pat come from?"

"Patricia. She was called Patricia when she was born. Now what's this bloody well got to do with fishing?"

"Patricia won't do either. It's too long."

"Flaming Nora!", said Jack. "Will you ever tell me what this malarkey is all about?"

"Nora. Now that'll work perfectly, Jack, as long as you don't mind using that in the formula. Pat need never know."

"Reilly, what formula are you prattling on about? Tell me now or you're going over the side."

"Jack, the Corrib trout are not the finest in the world for nothing. They're also the cutest and are highly sensitive. When they rise to an artificial fly, they sense it immediately and spit it out.

"To catch a trout on an artificial fly, you've got to strike like lightning. To catch a trout on a natural mayfly, however, you've got to give the trout a *biteen* longer. And it's that *biteen* longer that my Uncle Stiofáin identified with pinpoint, forensic and laser-like accuracy.

"Stiofáin was a great man for the ladies, and strictly in the pursuit of science, loved to take them fishing.

"When a trout would rise to his fly, he'd amorously declare 'Oh my darling' (whatever the name of the girl he had in the boat at the time) and then strike.

"He noticed that, with certain girls, he was more successful hooking fish than with others. When he was with an Anne or a Liz or a Jane – even a Joy – the company might be delectable, but the results were less than perfect.

"Similarly, when in the company of a Fiona or a Regina or a Jessica, they'd have a great time but the fishing was only mediocre.

"His favourite girls' names to fish with were Annie, Sarah and Zara. With girls like those, he became the best angler on the Corrib.

"You see, Jack, success at dapping is an exact science. Use a girl's name with just one syllable and you'll strike too fast. Use a girl's name with three syllables and you're too slow. But the sweet-spot is two syllables. It's that forensic."

Just then a large trout swirled around Jack's mount and gobbled the fly.

In the sweetest voice you ever heard, Jack crooned, "Oh my darling Nora".

Reilly never had to ask for another match ticket.

INSIGHTS

- Science and precision play important roles in business and success.
- Find the precise formula for success and watch your results blossom.
- Remember never to upstage your client.

QUESTION

- What's your formula for business?

4

THERE'S A DIFFERENCE BETWEEN VISION & SIGHT

Shoot for the Moon. You might get there.

Buzz Aldrin

If your dreams don't scare you, they're too small.

Richard Branson

Our main business is not to see what lies dimly in the distance, but to do what lies clearly at hand.

Thomas Carlyle

Helen Keller once poignantly declared that "the most pathetic person in all the world is someone with sight but no vision". Reilly always loved the pathos of that quotation, without ever fully realising what it meant.

That would change one Monday morning in 1993.

He was presenting a module on presentation skills to a team of Irish business people based in Voronezh in Russia.

Each Monday, he had the class present on an aspect of social or cultural life that they'd experienced in Russia over the weekend.

At the time, there was a flourishing trade in 'blind-dating', where Western people were introduced to Russian people.

This particular morning, two young graduates, Sean and Máirtín, both from *Conamara*, chose to recall their first experience of a joint blind-date in Russia.

"It was like this", says Séan. "Myself and Máirtín went to the hotel where we were to meet our two dates. Everything went to plan and we met the two as arranged.

"And I'll tell you now without one word of a lie: Máirtín's date was a vision; mine was a sight."

INSIGHTS

- This crude, if subtle, distinction, inspired Reilly to create two distinct types of goals in SMACHT: Moon Goals and Action Goals.

- **Moon Goals** represent what winning looks like. They are the big, aspirational, audacious, someday goals that excite you and scare you in equal measure.

- **Action Goals** represent waypoints towards your Moon Goal. They are more predictable, visible and achievable.

- A classic example of a Moon Goal is the 25 May, 1961 announcement by U.S. President John F. Kennedy, that the U.S. "should commit itself to achieving the goal, before this decade is out, of landing a man on the Moon and returning him safely to the Earth". When Kennedy said this, there was neither evidence that this could be achieved nor a plan for achieving it.

- An Action Goal towards achieving this might have been to "have an astronaut orbit the Moon safely and return to earth safely, within the year".
- Action Goals form an arc, over time, leading towards the Moon Goal and, at the same time, a set of go/no-go checkpoints as to whether the Moon Goal is achievable at all.
- In SMACHT, we define Action Goals in terms of a year, month, day and now.
- So, in order for a business to survive and thrive, you need ambitious, meaningful Moon Goals that both challenge and motivate. And a series of Action Goals that guide you along the way or help you to understand when you need to change course.

QUESTIONS

- What is your Moon Goal?
- What is your Year Goal (that will bring you to your Moon Goal)?
- What is your Monthly Goal (that will bring you to your Year Goal)?
- What is your Daily Goal (that will bring you to your Month Goal)?
- What will you do Now (to bring you to your Day Goal)?

5

THE POWER OF CHOICE

*Everything can be taken from a man but one thing:
the last of the human freedoms – to choose one's attitude in
any given set of circumstances.*

Viktor Frankl, *Man's Search for Meaning*

Choice, not chance, determines destiny.

Montaigne

*Everything you are today is a result of choices you made in the past.
Everything you will be in the future will be a result of
choices you are making now.*

Deepak Chopra

If the truth be told, Reilly would have loved to have done Medicine. He'd worked as a porter in the hospital during the summer holidays and he was passionately into healing and helping people.

He'd never shared that with anyone, with the exception of his Mother who inveigled it out of him under duress the Easter before the Leaving Cert. exams.

"You, a doctor!", she scoffed when she heard him. "Reilly, welcome to the real world. If you'd wanted to be a doctor, you'd have to have been studying for years for it, not playing football and acting the maggot. I know, because my friend's daughter has not gone outside the door for the last five years preparing for it.

"And anyway, no one from our side has ever been a doctor."

And she proved right. The only reason Reilly didn't do Medicine was that he didn't get the requisite points in the Leaving Certificate.

Reilly would never forget the August day the brown envelope arrived from the Central Applications Office with news of his future life. He'd surprised everyone by getting 56 points in the Leaving the previous Friday and that would have sufficed for Medicine the year before.

Devastatingly for him, the points had gone up to 60 that year and he was offered his second choice of Commerce.

Reilly was a born optimist, however, and resolved quickly to make the best of what life had dealt him. He quickly discarded thoughts of Medicine and figured that maybe Commerce was meant for him. He put a smile on his face and repaired to the Cellar Bar where he regaled all and sundry on the benefits of Commerce.

Four of Reilly's buddies also didn't get the points for Medicine that summer. All of them are doctors today. How so?

Two of them chose to repeat the Leaving to gain the additional points. Another chose to go the scenic route and did a BSc before going on to do Medicine. The fourth wouldn't have gotten the points to do Medicine in Ireland had he been doing the Leaving 'til now. But he chose to persist with his dream and discovered that, at that time, the qualification criteria to study medicine in the UK was based on a modicum of academic points combined with bedside manner skills. He is now a most successful gynaecologist in Derby.

It would be many years later before Reilly assimilated the learning from that experience.

INSIGHTS

- The common denominator between all five outcomes was choice. Reilly chose to accept what society had offered him. His buddies refused to do that and instead chose to follow their own desires.

- You are a choice-making machine. From the moment you awake in the morning to when you sleep at night, you are engaged in one series of choices after another. Whether you spring out of bed or press the snooze button is a choice. Whether you wear the pink shirt or the white or the blue is a choice. The way you go to work, whether consciously or mostly unconsciously, is a choice. The way you treat people is a choice.

- Tellingly, who you become as a person is also a choice. Jim Rohn observed that every life form seems to strive to its maximum, except human beings. "How tall will a tree grow? As tall as it possibly can. Human beings on the other hand have been given the dignity of choice. Each of us has two distinct choices to make about what we do with our lives. The first choice is to be less than we have the capacity to be. To earn less. To have less. To read less and to think less. And the second choice? To do it all. To become all that we can possibly be."

- The power in choice happens when you become conscious of your choices. Unlike his buddies, Reilly wasn't even aware or conscious that he had a choice when he got those Leaving Cert. results.

QUESTIONS

- What sort of person will you choose to be?
- What sort of business will you choose to create?
- What sort of contribution will you choose to make?

6

THE CISTERCIAN WAY

*The two most important days in your life are the day
you are born and the day you find out why.*

Mark Twain

*Two roads diverged in a wood, and I—
I took the one less traveled by,
And that has made all the difference.*

Robert Frost

Tony Hogan was every bit the golden-eyed boy. In September 1951, he was elected House Captain of Cistercian College Roscrea by his fellow students. This is the ultimate peer accolade.

Later that year, together with Gerry Culliton, he would man the front row of a marauding Roscrea pack that beat all before it in Leinster and Munster schools rugby.

Months later, he captained the athletic team to win the All-Ireland. He himself was national shot-put champion and held the national record for years after.

And whilst not as flamboyant an orator as Gus Martin, he participated with him on a debating team that beguiled audiences in convent halls in Banagher and the Bower and Bunclody.

Those young men surely had the world as their oyster as they departed the hallowed halls of Roscrea College.

Gerry and Gus both took right turns at the College front door. They were beckoned by the bright lights of Dublin and the allure of bigger stages.

In the years that followed, Gerry would win 19 senior rugby caps for Ireland and the Barbarians. To this day, he has the unique distinction of being the only Irish rugby forward ever to be capped in the front row, the second row and back row.

Gus would become professor of English in UCD and inspire several generations of Irish students through his iconic books: *Exploring English* and *Soundings*.

Tony was called in a different direction. He took a road less travelled. He took a left turn at the College front door and walked the 100 short yards from the College to Mount St. Joseph Abbey.

He took the Cistercian Way – becoming 'Fr. Flannan' in the process.

Becoming a contemplative monk would enable him pursue his calling and purpose in life: the love of Latin. His only distraction for the rest of his life would be the students in his *alma mater*.

Reilly was one of those distractions and remembers to this day his first Latin class in 2B.

Fr. Flannan entered the class quietly and proceeded to write two words on the blackboard in chalk. Reilly can still see them: *Ad vitam.*

Fr. Flannan beamed beatifically at the class of 2B and whispered: "No doubt you've heard the adage that:

Latin is a language as dead as dead can be.
It killed the Romans long ago and now it's killing me.

"Well, my goal is to ad vitam: to bring Latin 'to life' for you.

"And your goal is to get an 'A' in Latin in the Inter. Certificate in three years' time."

And he then uttered a little whistle of satisfaction beneath his breath that sounded like "Coo-Coo". It was a custom of his that he did any time he made a point that pleased him. Everyone in Roscrea had a nickname and, for this reason, Fr. Flannan was only ever called 'The Pigeon', or more affectionately, 'The Pidge'.

Ad vitam were the first two Latin words Reilly learned. Later, they would become much more than words: they would become a manifesto to live life by.

The Pidge believed that it was possible to bring to life whatever you were focused on and, indeed, that our purpose in life was to do so. And to this end, his classes were a sanctuary of learning and discovery and joy.

Reilly remembers another day.

"Anyone know where the word 'tractor' derives from?", says The Pidge.

It was a well targeted question. At least half of the class came from good farming stock and had as much, if not more, interest in tractors than girls. They were quick to boost their preferred tractor manufacturers.

"Hino", says Richie Cahill enthusiastically.

"Massey Ferguson", says Mike O'Flynn.

"Zetor", says Martin Kelly.

The Pidge coo-coo'd with delight. He had the class in the palm of his hand.

When the banter abated, The Pidge explained that the word tractor derived from the Latin word 'tracere' which means 'to pull' or 'to pull towards'.

As he pirouetted around and back to the class, he noticed John Ball staring off out towards the playing pitches.

The Pidge paused and allowed the class to settle.

"You seem a bit distracted, John?", The Pidge said gently.

"You're spot on, Father. I'm from Louisburg and I'm out of my mind thinking about Mayo not having won an All Ireland since 1951. It's all I think about most days. I live in a state of total distraction."

This was in 1972.

The Pidge sauntered back up to the blackboard and wrote the word 'GOAL' in a large circle on the right-hand side of the blackboard.

"What's our GOAL, boys?"

"To get an 'A' in Latin in the Inter."

"Excellent. Boys, in the pursuit of any worthy goal in life, always remember that there are forces pulling you towards your goal; pulling you away from your goal; and keeping you stuck where you are.

"All three forces have their origin in the word 'TRACERE'.

"TRACTION are those forces that will pull you towards your goal.

"PROCRASTINATION are those forces that prevent you moving now.

"DISTRACTION are those forces that drag you away from your goal."

John Ball listened attentively to The Pidge that day and banished Mayo football from his mind. And although he would come first in Latin in the entire country in his Inter. Cert, he'd still trade it for just one All Ireland.

INSIGHTS

- Your big stage may not necessarily be Carnegie Hall or Croke Park. Your big stage is wherever you are. Right now.
- Purpose trumps goals in business and life every time.
- You're happiest and most fulfilled when you're living on purpose.
- Keep asking yourself what you're doing when you're happiest and most fulfilled. And do that all day long. That will be your purpose.
- Have clear goals for yourself, your clients and your team.
- Be aware of the myriad distractions in your life.

- Traction pulls you towards your goals. Distraction pulls you away. Procrastination keeps you stuck. Choose your force consciously.
- Take the road less travelled.

QUESTIONS

- What's your purpose in business and life?
- What are your goals for yourself, your family and your clients?

7

A PARADIGM SHIFT

---

*A simple paradigm shift is all it takes to change the
course of your life forever.*

Jeff Spires

*Everybody is a genius. But if you judge a fish by its ability
to climb a tree, it will live its whole life believing it's stupid.*

Albert Einstein

Reilly had spent most of the preceding 24 hours celebrating Ireland's victory over the old enemy and he was now as sick as a small hospital. Mercifully, the train was almost deserted and so he hunkered down to get some badly-needed sleep.

That all changed utterly in Tullamore.

A man arrived into the carriage with four kids, aged from about three to 10, and they were ballistic. They were shouting; they were roaring; they were fighting. And all the while, the man just stared out the window at the uninspiring Bog of Allen, and literally did nothing.

Reilly managed to keep a lid on it until one of the kids started pegging paper airplanes at him and laughed gleefully when one connected with Reilly's eye.

Reilly had it. He marched over to the man and, bending closely to his ear so no one else could hear him, he said: "Now listen carefully to me. I've had a brewery load of porter over the past day and I'm in no mood to tolerate the ructions your kids are causing. Now are you going to talk to them, or am I?"

The man looked kindly at Reilly and said: "Their Mother died a few hours ago in Tullamore Hospital and I just don't know how to break it to them".

Reilly understood for the first time what a paradigm shift was.

INSIGHTS

- The dictionary defines a paradigm shift as 'an important change that happens when the usual way of thinking about or doing something is replaced by a new and different way.'
- It is important to have paradigm shifts from time to time in the way we think about ourselves, our way of life, and our business.

QUESTION

- What paradigm shifts do you need to have as a person and as a business?

8

FIND YOUR LIGHTHOUSE

There are times when the ocean is not the ocean
— not blue, not even water, but some violent explosion of
energy and danger: ferocity on a scale only Gods can
summon. It hurls itself at the island, sending spray right
over the top of the lighthouse, biting pieces off the cliff.
And the sound is a roaring of a beast whose anger knows no
limits. Those are the nights the light is needed most.

M.L. Stedman, *The Light Between Oceans*

Pádraig Ó Céidigh is forever counselling Reilly on the importance, in aviation and in business, of 'being able to fly with instruments, and without instruments'.

It was pithy and salutary advice for Reilly mid-way through the annual Frances Thornton Memorial Galway Bay Swim last Saturday.

The swim, from Aughinish in County Clare to Blackrock Diving Tower in Salthill, Galway, is one of the longest open-water swims in Ireland and is the only bay swim crossing on the Wild Atlantic Way.

Reilly had the great privilege of escorting Lisa Dunne, the wonderful Sligo swimmer, by boat across a choppy Galway Bay.

Both were clear on their roles. Reilly was expected to track a course as close as possible to that set out by the Navionics Marine Global Positioning System he was using. Lisa was expected to be guided by Reilly and win her class in the swim.

Things began swimmingly!

A kind south-westerly wind boded favourably for swimmers and boaters alike. Then abruptly, the wind veered westerly and began to hurl the swimmers at the boats. Then it veered to a *gaoth aniar aduaigh* (the dreaded north-westerly) and began to slap the swimmers into their faces.

Reilly was at the pin of his Helly Hansen collar to keep the RIB positioned on the course of the GPS. And he would have too, only that the battery charge suddenly died in his mobile phone powering it.

Lisa wasn't to know it then – or indeed later – but she was swimming without instruments.

Fortunately, for centuries, mariners have sought out and discovered exotic places around the world through the aid of wonderful structures called lighthouses. And Reilly had been brought up looking out at both of the lighthouses on Galway Bay: Mutton Island and Blackhead.

In fact, he knew that, by lining them up with the red lights on top of the transmitter mast on the Tonabrocky transmitting station, it would very nearly bring him in the front door of the ladies' changing rooms in Blackrock.

Despite eight miles of pounding seas, there wasn't as much as a cigarette paper between the top three swimmers.

After the celebrations had abated that evening in the Salthill Hotel, Lisa confided to Reilly: "What won it for us was superior technology. The course GPS shows that we travelled a slightly straighter line – and *ergo* less of a distance – than the other swimmers. Them's the small margins, Reilly. We had the more modern technology!"

Reilly thought of Ó Céidigh but said nothing.

Reilly has visited many beautiful sites throughout Ireland and the world. But he's especially drawn to sites, that although beautiful in their own way, are more about function than aesthetics.

Reilly loves lighthouses.

INSIGHTS

- Modern navigation technologies, such as GPS, have made lighthouses less of a factor in today's sea travel, although hundreds are still in operation. What will never go out of fashion, however, are the three things a lighthouse provides to travellers: light; hope; and safety.

- A lighthouse is a wonderful metaphor for life and business. There are two ways of looking at them: when we are lost at sea or floundering near rocks, and losing hope, it is the lighthouse in our life that brings us home; and when we see another in need of our support, care or guidance, we can shine a light to help guide them back home. This magic of reciprocation is at the very core of human kindness. At any time of life, we can either need, or be, a lighthouse.

- Deep within each of us is an even deeper calling for why we choose this particular path on the voyage of our lives. Watch carefully for it quietly beckoning to you like a bright light in the storm. If you can find your lighthouse, you can find your way.

QUESTIONS

- **Light:** Do you have a clear vision for yourself and your business that is clear for all to see and navigate towards?
- **Hope:** Do you maintain a positive expectancy of success?
- **Safety:** Do you identify important white elephants in the room and make it safe for people to discuss them openly?

9

THE ULTIMATE
DISCIPLINE OF
EXECUTION

Ar scáth a chéile a mhaireann na daoine.
(People survive and thrive by helping each other.)

Irish proverb

R eilly often felt sorry for Charles Mitchell as he solemnly delivered the weather forecast after the 9 o'clock evening news.

Even as an innocent nine-year-old, he realised it wasn't Mitchell's fault that the prevailing weather conditions of the west of Ireland more often than not promised heavy rain.

His country cousins were not impressed, however, and would proceed to project a tirade of abuse at the newsreader.

This evening was particularly tense.

For seven full days since the hay was cut, it had rained the proverbial cats and dogs and the sodden crop was now ominously turning an unhealthy shade of green. Nobody dared make a sound as the morrow's weather ultimatum was read.

"A rapidly moving anticyclone will cross Ireland over the next 24 hours. It will be accompanied by temperatures of 24 degrees Celsius in a moderate to fresh south-westerly breeze. This will be followed by a system of low pressure, bringing with it persistent and thundery downpours for most of the coming week."

Reilly's cousin, Paddy Coen, took what seemed an eternity to reflect on the forecast. Dragging deeply on an untipped Sweet Afton, he exhaled profusely into the open turf fire before proclaiming with certainty and conviction.

"We'll have the *Meitheal* tomorrow. Take the bike and do the rounds. Call on the Connellys, the Beattys, the Egans, the Corcorans, the Culkeens, the Burkes and the Reddingtons and tell them the *Meitheal* begins after 7 o'clock breakfast tomorrow morning."

Reilly, being the youngest, was summarily dispatched to announce the news of the impending *Meitheal*.

"There's a *Meitheal* in Coens' tomorrow morning at seven sharp."

Being a city lad, he had no idea what a *Meitheal* was but it sure was whipping up one hell of a storm with the neighbours.

He awoke the following morning to an explosion of senses. The kitchen was bursting at the seams with representations from each of the neighbouring families. There was already a tangible and giddy exuberance building amongst them. Even Mr. Conway, the County Solicitor, who rented land from his cousins, had arrived to partake and was tucking into his breakfast with gusto.

Following the breakfast, Reilly watched on fascinated as his shy, docile and retiring cousin Paddy metamorphosed before his eyes.

He now stood at the top of the kitchen table, and like generations before him, he connected with his tribe.

Placing a single leaf of blue Belvedere Bond notepaper beside him, he began, "Today, we will dry and save all the hay in the Race Park field".

There were loud cheers and shouts whilst Paddy waited patiently for them to abate. (The 'What'. Clear Goal)

"As the weather is due to change later tonight, it's an absolute must that we get the hay in the Race Park dried and under cocks by this evening. Failure to do so would result in us losing the entire crop and would leave us with no fodder for the winter."

The message was greeted with the *gravitas* it merited, even by the smart-asses in the group. It had now transformed from being a dream to a mission. (The 'Why'. Rationale.)

"We'll begin at 8am sharp and aim to have the first, and heaviest, turning done by noon. We'll have a rest for a while and then get the second turning done by 4pm. The third and final turning should take us no more than two hours which means we should have the hay as dry as a bone by 7pm. We'll then stack it in cocks, cover them with *cáipeen*s and be ready to begin the party by 10 o'clock." (Clear schedule of events.)

There was an animated response to Paddy's plan. Some felt it was too optimistic; others felt it could be done quicker or better or more easily. Paddy listened attentively to each suggestion and allowed each person time to have their say. It seemed to Reilly that the *Meitheal* was descending into chaos with the amount and diversity of opinions and ideas. (Always involve the group in coming up with innovative solutions.)

Reilly thought Waterloo was well and truly lost when Mickeen Culkeen, who was only five years older than him, asked enthusiastically: "Why don't we make a game out of the hay making?"

There was pandemonium. Some of the elders accused him of being immature and not taking things seriously. Paddy moved swiftly to protect him, however.

"What's behind your question, Mick?'"

Mick knew he was under the spotlight – but that's where he performed best.

"I've just counted the number of hay turners in the room and there's 16 of us. Let's divide the Big Field into 16 equal squares and have a race to see who finishes first."

Paddy sketched out 16 squares in pencil on a sheet of brown paper. (The Scoreboard.)

The focus now wasn't on the plan. That was a *fait accomplit* that had already been bought into. It now was on who would get what square. (Commitment.)

They couldn't get out to the Big Field quick enough. The games had well and truly begun. (Commitment and Accountability.)

Reilly was surprised that Paddy elected not to turn a wisp of hay that day, even though he was acknowledged as a legendary man with a rake and a sure contender to win the competition.

"There are days to work *in* the hay and other days to work *on* the hay. Today, Reilly, is a day to work on the hay", said Paddy quietly. "Our only job today is to make it easier for others to do theirs."

And that's what they did. They supported those 16 hay turners as if their lives depended on it. They covered miles ferrying milky, sugary tea in Lucozade bottles to every turner.

Reilly observed Paddy checking in with each turner and giving them feedback on their performance. (Freed up the team to work on the main thing and prevent them being distracted by the whirlwind of day-to-day activities.)

Peter Gleeson, Reilly's cousin, who'd played football for Dublin in Wembley earlier that year, was fit as a fiddle and bolted into an early lead that morning. Gradually, however, the slower but steadier rhythm of the Reddington brothers won out in the end and they finished marginally in front, just before 11.30am. In the spirit of the *Meitheal*, they now proceeded to help Mr. Conway, who despite having the fanciest of rakes and forks, was struggling with both the pace and the rising heat. (Measurement, Tracking, Keeping Score, Helping Strugglers.)

Slowly and perceptibly, the colour of the Big Field changed. By noon, the once-turned hay stood fluffier and yellower than earlier. By mid-afternoon, as the temperature continued to soar and the fresh wind provided the best of drying conditions, the hay turned a straw-white shade. By evening time, the hay was ready for cocking and, by 9 pm, the big field had been transformed from a carpet of sodden hay to an assortment of gaily-capped hay cocks.

Reilly learned afterwards that it had been a great party. He'd fallen asleep first, and not surprisingly awoke first the following morning.

It was like as if nothing had happened the day before. The kitchen was deserted but spotless and had returned to its former order. He peeked out the window to confirm that they'd actually saved the hay. And they had. Although it was raining a lake outside, the freshly-made cocks were as dry as corks.

The only evidence that a *Meitheal* had occurred lay neatly on the tidy kitchen table. The brown sheet of paper was somewhat the worse for wear but finishing times and final positions, 1 to 16, had been completed.

Beside it lay the single sheet of blue Belvedere Bond notepaper with Paddy's handwritten notes for the *Meitheal*.

INSIGHTS

- *Meitheal*s work because they are based on the simple notion that the whole is greater than the sum of the parts.

- Every successful *Meitheal* has someone appointed who 'makes it easier for others to do their jobs'. The Latin word for 'to make easy' is 'facile'. The role of a 'facilitator' is 'to make things easier'. Every great organisation has a great facilitator at its core.

- There are six words that every great facilitator lives by. The only notes scribbled on Paddy's blue sheet were the immortal lines of Kipling:

I keep six honest serving men.
They taught me all I knew.
Their names are What and Why and When
Where and How and Who.

- Every *Meitheal* has one clear outcome and all activity is focused on it and all other distractions are deflected away from it.

- Everyone is crystal clear on what's expected of them.

- Everyone has the right materials to do the job.

- There is a scorecard, created by the team, that highlights where exactly the team are and where exactly each member of the team is and how they're performing.

- There is a culture of the strong helping the weak.

- In the Celtic calendar, *Meitheal*s were held seasonally or quarterly. The notion of a quarterly strategy *Meitheal* is one of the most powerful concepts in organisational change management.
- Execution is the core responsibility of the business leader. The *Meitheal* is the ultimate execution tool.

QUESTIONS

- Do you have a quarterly *Meitheal* in your business?

MARKETING

10

HOW THE JAPS BOMBED
BELL HARBOUR

If you confuse, you lose.

Don Millar

Reilly's Uncle Stiofáin operated a thriving transatlantic business out of *Conamara* in the 1930s and 1940s. He would supply the four harbours of South Galway Bay – Kinvara; New Quay; Bell Harbour; and Ballyvaughan – with turf from *Conamara*, and return laden down with the finest potatoes in the world from North Clare.

It was symbiotic barter at its best.

And it wasn't just turf and spuds that were traded. Information of both the micro and macro variety was exchanged and robustly debated in the safe and salubrious hostelries in each of the harbours.

One fair and clement day in December 1941, Stiofáin lurched the *Gleoteog* on her side in New Quay and the crew began unloading and loading cargo for the imminent Christmas season.

This would be the time he would repair to Linnane's Hostelry and have a 'Transatlantic Summit' with his great and wise friend, Bridie Gaynor, the *Bean an Tí*.

"*Bail ó Dhia ar an obair* (God bless the work)", boomed Stiofáin cheerfully to Bridie and some of the local lads sitting at the bar, getting into practice for the festive season.

"*Aon scéal*? (Any news?)"

"Gerry Sweeney is after landing a sky-blue coloured lobster and he's at least four feet from claw to claw. I bet ye never saw the likes of that beyond in *Conamara*", said one of the lads boastfully.

People listened carefully for Stiofáin's response because his opinion on maritime matters was revered.

"*Anam an Diabhaill!* (The Devil's soul!) I've heard tell of a sky-blue lobster landed off Aran but I never yet laid eyes on one myself. That's indeed a great feat."

"And one of Annie Nolan's hens has taken to laying bright pink eggs", said someone else.

"I've seen pink eggs myself in my time, and if I have itself, I'll wager a shilling she's got a rooster called Gay. We threw him out of *Conamara* years ago."

Even the Burren lads couldn't restrain themselves from laughing out loud at Stiofáin's riposte.

What with the banter and the craic, Bridie was finding it hard to listen to the one o'clock news on the transistor radio as was her wont.

It didn't, however, prevent her from getting the gist of it – and that was all that mattered.

"Whisht", she says, with terror in her voice. "I think ·they're after bombing Bell Harbour."

You could have heard a pin drop in the pub.

There wasn't a person among them who wasn't related to or knew someone in Bell Harbour, a bare two miles away.

And there wasn't one amongst them who didn't rely in one way or another on the sea for their livelihoods.

Bridie's was the only radio in the parish at the time, and as there were no phones either, it was up to the clientele of that pub to go forth and break the news.

Most did so by shank's mare. Those that had bicycles ventured farther afield with the news. Stiofáin made the full eight mile transatlantic crossing of Galway Bay aboard his Galway Hooker.

The quay at Spiddal was, as they say, *lán go doras* (full to the door) when Stiofáin berthed the *Gleoteog*.

They'd come in their slews to get their paws on the exotic *liathróidí plúr* (balls of flour) from New Quay that would adorn the Christmas table with every meal over the festive period.

Stiofáin knew the importance of clarity of communications and saw this as the ideal opportunity to deliver one message to as many people as possible.

Standing tall on the gunwale of the *Gleoteog*, he called for whisht and didn't utter a syllable until he got it.

"I've just returned from across the sea in County Clare and I regret to inform you that the Japs have bombed Bell Harbour. If they've done this to the kind and gentle people of Bell Harbour, there's no telling what they'll stop at.

"Go immediately and inform – in particular – anyone who might be living on their own. Tell them, if possible, to sleep tonight with a metal lid over their heads."

Such was the effectiveness of that communication process that, for years afterwards, many of the good people of *Conamara* could be found sleeping with tin or metal lids over their heads.

And that's how the people of Ireland got to hear about how the Japs bombed Bell Harbour on 7 December, 1941.

INSIGHTS

- Words, like bombs, can be used to both kill or to transform. The slightest alteration to a word – even one letter – can change utterly the meaning and the impact of that word and message.
- In matters of life and death, the gist of the message is not nearly enough. You need accurate details.
- Equally, it's critical to check the source of your information.
- Although the quality of radios has improved greatly over the years, there is more interference now than ever. Imagine how much clearer your reception of the world would be today if you switched off Facebook and Twitter and Instagram, even for the weekend!
- The quality and clarity of your marketing messages are, believe it or not, a matter of business life and death – your business's life or death.

QUESTIONS

- Can your website pass the 'Grunt Test'? If a caveman was to look at your website and asked to grunt if they could tell (a) what it is you sell; (b) how it will benefit them; and (c) how they can buy it, would they grunt enthusiastically?
- When someone asks you, either in business, or socially, "What do you do?", can you answer them clearly, confidently and compellingly?
- Do your team clearly know your vision, values and mission? In fact, do you?

11

HOT LEADS

*If you concentrate on the activities of prospecting,
presenting and following up,
the sales will look after themselves.*

Brian Tracy

Bless me, Father, for I have sinned. I have been with a feisty girl", confessed Reilly peevishly.

"Is that you, Reilly?", asked the priest knowingly.

"Yes, Father, I regret to say it's me."

"And who was this girl you were with?"

"I can't tell you that, Father. I wish to protect her reputation."

"Well, Reilly, I'm sure to find her name out sooner or later so you may as well tell me. By any chance, was it Sarah Kelly?"

"I can't tell you, Father."

"Was it Fiona Larkin?"

"I'm sorry, but I will not name her."

"Was it Therese Allen?"

"I will not say."

"Well, was it Regina Power then?"

"My lips are sealed."

Reilly heard the priest heave a deep sigh of frustration.

"Reilly, I must say that you have your principles and for that I admire you. But in the eyes of the church, you have sinned, and so you must atone. You are summarily precluded from all altar boy activities for the next three months."

Reilly sidled back to his pew where Flaherty was eagerly awaiting news on his penance.

"What d'ya get, Reilly?"

"Three months holidays and four hot leads."

INSIGHTS

- Always remember that you're only ever one conversation away from a life-changing experience – but that's not likely to happen behind a computer screen.

- The gold prospectors of old knew that there was 'gold in them there hills'. That's where the phrase 'sales prospecting' derived from.

- Prospecting is the fuel that drives sales. Great salespeople are constantly searching for hot prospects and leads.

- Ensure that your pipeline is always awash with quality prospects.

- Schedule time for holidays now. It's the time when you reinvent and recreate and rejuvenate.

QUESTIONS

- How many quality prospects have you in your pipeline?
- How many quality prospects did you tell your story to last week?
- How many quality prospects will you tell your story to this week?

12

THE ULTIMATE SALES QUESTION

*In selling, as in medicine,
prescription before diagnosis is malpractice.*

Tony Allasandra

R eilly was fierce proud to address a group of entrepreneurs at the magnificent Engine Collaboration Centre in Limerick for the start of National Enterprise Week on behalf of LEO Limerick.

It brought him back 30 years to his first sales experience.

Reilly had just teamed up with Envision Marketing to begin promoting training as a string to their bow.

Envision was the brainchild of Jim Ward and Aidan Daly, who had pioneered the teaching and practice of marketing principles in the West of Ireland. So many dynamic businesses like Chanelle, Dubarry's and Cashback bear the fingerprints of Jim and Aidan.

Reilly had succeeded in getting a sales appointment with Ned Toomey, the head of the newly-formed Limerick County Enterprise Board (CEB). He'd arranged that he and Aidan Daly, who was easily Ireland's best sales trainer, would meet Ned at 4pm in his office one Friday afternoon.

Things were going swimmingly until they came upon a traffic accident on the Ennis Road and ended up arriving 20 minutes late for the meeting. As this was a time before mobile phones, and coin boxes that worked, there was no way of alerting Ned to their late arrival.

In his anxiety, Reilly couldn't wait to get out of the car and into the meeting as fast as possible.

Aidan, however, restrained him and, taking out his writing pad, asked Reilly a question: "Reilly, what would make this a great meeting?"

"Aidan, we're dead late. We need to just get to that meeting before we're any later."

But Aidan wasn't for budging and repeated the question: "Reilly, what would make this a great meeting?"

Reilly realised there was no way out other than to answer the question. He had to dig deep to focus on it.

"It would be great if we simply got to know who Ned Toomey is and put a face to the name."

Aidan began scribbling on his notepad.

"What else, Reilly?"

"As the CEBs are a new Government initiative, it'd be great to establish what their remit really is and what specifically they plan in doing and what their challenges are in implementing that work.

"And what would be really great is if we could walk out with a day's work just to show them what great sales trainers we are – even if we have to do that free."

Aidan made a few notes of his own before summarising to Reilly:

Outcomes for the Meeting.

- Get to know Ned really well by finding things in common with him.
- Find out what Limerick CEB's plans for training are this year and in addition, what the plans are for the entire country.
- Establish what their concerns and challenges are in carrying out and implementing the training.
- Set a date for a training session where we can provide an excellent experience at a great fee.

Before they had time to take their seats, Aidan had established that both he and Ned had worked in a former life with Shannon Development. For the next 10 minutes, they regaled each other with tales of Brendan O'Regan, whom they both revered and agreed had been one of the great national heroes of economic development in the region.

This segued effortlessly into question 2 where Ned outlined his economic development plan for the Limerick region. He believed its success would be entirely dependent on providing indigenous entrepreneurs with the attitude, skills and accountability to create and grow profitable businesses.

His major concern, however, was that there was nobody sufficiently capable of delivering all this training together. He wanted one provider to deliver strategic, marketing, financial and systems training and provide it as a single management development programme.

He revealed that the heads of every CEB in the country were meeting in Miltown Malbay in a month's time to debate and discuss the challenge.

When Aidan proposed they present a model to all the CEBs that he had pioneered successfully for Invest Northern Ireland, Ned beamed like the cat who'd gotten the cream.

That one super-meeting 30 years ago spawned an entire industry of leadership, management and retail development programmes that Reilly still continues to deliver to this day.

INSIGHTS

- Never, ever, ever attend a meeting of any description without first asking yourself the super-question: What would make this a great meeting?
- Be aware of the average life value of every client. Clients like the calibre of Ned, and many of his contemporaries in the CEBs, can be life-long customers provided you treat them excellently.
- Never, ever, ever sell without first creating rapport. You win rapport by finding things in common with your prospect. Or as Dale Carnegie counselled so many years ago in his iconic book, *How to Win Friends and Influence People*: "Be interested rather than interesting". It's still one of the great truisms of the selling game that people buy people first and your products or services after.
- Aidan once trained Reilly to picture the four letters MMFI emblazoned on a customer's forehead. They stand for MAKE ME FEEL IMPORTANT and any time you make a customer feel important enhances massively the potential for progress.
- Follow the process that doctors do: Examine; diagnose; prescribe – in that order.

QUESTIONS

- What would make this a great meeting?
- What is the average life value (ALV) of your top clients?
- Who are you more focused on during a sales meeting: Yourself or your customer? The answer may explain your results.

TRIBUTE

Professor Jim Ward and Dr. Aidan Daly, apart from being pioneering marketing academics and practitioners, were first and foremost servants to their students.

Everything they aspired to had their students front and centre. Nothing pleased them more than to see their students succeed and they'd move mountains to ensure that happened.

Aidan drove Reilly to his first job as a marketing executive in Heritage Knitwear in Castlebar in 1983.

When Mrs. Reilly landed an interview for a senior sales role in Galway Crystal straight out of university, Jim met the American Directors of the company and assured them that, whilst she didn't have the requisite three years' experience, she more than made up for it in potential. She got the job and nailed it.

When Reilly and Mrs. Reilly's son, Shane, completed his Master's in Marketing, both Jim and Aidan, although retired, showed up for the graduation to be there and support.

Because Jim and Aidan were always interested in their students.

There's an invaluable lesson there for all of us in business and life.

13

YOUR #1 ADVANTAGE
IN BUSINESS

Find a growing market.
Growing markets are like a tailwind:
they make everything move forward faster.
Declining markets are like headwinds:
they make all efforts harder.

Alex Hormozi

R eilly learned much about creating a seriously profitable business on his first day of 2nd Commerce in UCG in 1980. The only trouble was that he didn't realise it at the time – and most certainly didn't apply it. Shaw wasn't far wide of the mark when he quipped: "Wisdom is wasted on the old and youth is wasted on the young".

"If you were going to open a burger stand, and you could only have one advantage over your competitors … what would it be?"

At a time when students were more used to being lectured to, this Socratic approach to learning was almost disarming.

There was a myriad of suggestions from the 150-strong lecture theatre: "Location! … Quality! …. Low prices! ….Great taste! … "Curry sauce".

Professor Jim Ward, as was his wont, let it go round the houses until eventually the students ran out of answers. Theatrically, he then uncovered a slide with just three words: A STARVING CROWD.

"Think about it", said Jim. "You could have exorbitant prices, terrible burgers, and be in the middle of a field but, if you're the only burger stand when the Pope comes to town – he had earlier that year – you're going to sell out."

It reminded Reilly of an incident at the Rose of Tralee earlier that month.

Reilly, and a slew of Roscrea buddies, would descend on 'the beautiful vale of Tralee' each year for the annual festival. Midway through the first night, Tarps arrived back into the pub with the biggest candy floss Reilly had ever seen.

"Where did ya get that?", says Reilly, who was born with a sweet tooth.

"Some fella from Kiltullagh is down a side street and he's churning them out to beat the band", says Tarps.

Reilly observed the candy floss man closely as he stood in line. He was broad-shouldered, and he seemed to have endless energy and enthusiasm with a chat for everyone. He looked mildly intellectual, if it wasn't that he was a 'candy floss man'.

"You have a way with people", says Reilly, as he waited for his candy floss.

"It's the day job", says the candy floss man, "but I've found it's great for business. If you're nice to people, they'll come back to you time after time."

"You're a social worker?"

"I'm a Principal of a National School."

"Pull the other one", says Reilly.

"I will", says the candy floss man. "If you bring three of your buddies back here, I'll pull you a free candy floss for yourself. And I'll only charge you today's prices. The price goes up again tomorrow, as I've discovered there's a lot of hungry people here."

On 21 June last, Reilly interviewed Pat McDonagh, the MD and founder of Supermac's, before an audience of the good and the great of the Limerick business community in the Castletroy Hotel.

Reilly has done this several times in the past and always ends the session with this question: "Pat, you operate in excess of 300 separate businesses, across a variety of industries, almost all of them highly profitable. What is the most profitable business you ever operated?"

"Reilly, the most profitable business I ever ran was selling candy floss on my school holidays at various festivals around the country.

"There was almost an insatiable demand for the pink sugar on a stick that I sold for 50p a shot. I calculated that the material cost of the sugar and the stick was less than 2p a shot; the machine I used was a Kenwood cake mixer borrowed from my mother; the rent and rates were free; and the labour was my own.

"That, Reilly, was the most profitable business I ever operated."

INSIGHTS

- Find a starving crowd: They're everywhere.
- Make them irresistible offers.
- Wage an ongoing and relentless war on costs: Many of us learned how possible this is during Covid.
- Raise the prices of at least one of your products or service: As Dan Kennedy famously said, "There is no strategic benefit to being the second cheapest in the marketplace, but there is for being the most expensive".

QUESTIONS

- How hungry are your crowd?
- How irresistible are your offers?
- What's your ambition?

POSTSCRIPT

Jim Ward regularly emphasised the power and importance of names in communication and marketing. Reilly always admired the way he changed the name of The Marketing Department in UCG to The Marketing Discipline. That's SMACHT.

14

THE IMPORTANCE OF A GOOD QUALIFICATION

I had no education. I had to use my brains.

Bill Shanley

When Reilly was a nipper growing up in Galway, you'd never hear tell of the likes of a psychiatrist or a psychologist or a therapist or a counsellor.

There was no need for one, because of Tim O'Shea.

Tim ran a barber's emporium behind Cahill's drapery shop on Williamsgate Street and was visited upon by the good and the great of the city. Locals will tell you that they never can recall a time when there wasn't a queue out the door for Tim. If he wasn't the best barber in Galway itself, he certainly was the busiest.

Many speculated as to his secret.

Some said it was location. The reality was, however, that if you found him at all, you took your life in your hands navigating the rickety stairs up to the first floor salon.

Others said it must have been the signage and merchandising. Tim wouldn't even agree to a barber's pole outside the premises.

One bright spark speculated that Tim might have had superior hairdressing qualifications to his competitors.

Tim's only concession to corporate trappings, however, was a sober-looking business card affixed to the corner of the mirror. Written in the solid black font of the time, it simply said: "Tim O'Shea. N.H.Q.W."

Whilst it confounded several visiting academics, Tim would never be drawn on what the qualification was or where he had acquired it.

To the eight-year-old Reilly, however, Tim's success was as obvious as the nose on your face. People always emerged from Tim feeling better about themselves than when they entered.

As a kid, it always intrigued Reilly to see Tim play the 'Stars Game'.

Above the mirror were three large framed black-and-white photographs from left to right of John Wayne, Elvis Presley, and George Best. When a client was comfortably seated, Tim would ask them confidentially which 'Star' they'd most like to look like.

Many took an age to decide yet Tim never hurried them.

What fascinated the young Reilly was that, irrespective of who they said they'd like to look like, Tim always delivered the same haircut – a short back and sides.

It was the only style he knew.

And even though every customer came out of Tim's with the exact same hair style, the kids playing football out in Manifold's yard could predict with absolute certainty what style they'd ordered.

Those that had a 'John Wayne' always emerged pretending to shoot you. Those that had an 'Elvis' would inevitably come out crooning *You Ain't Nothing but a Hound-dog* and those that had a 'George Best' would invariably try to dribble the ball around you.

Tim may not have had the most salubrious salon in town or the most dexterous fingers with a scissors but he had a wonderful process to generate profitable business.

His business was built upon one qualification that isn't always taught in university curricula.

Tim made everyone who entered his business feel important and special.

INSIGHTS

- You don't necessarily need the best product or service in town to flourish.
- People only ever buy two things: solutions to problems and good feelings. Tim delivered both in spades.
- Dale Carnegie once counselled that the key to interpersonal success is: MOFI – Make Others Feel Important. Tim O'Shea lived and died by this maxim.
- Joe Coyle teaches people to get to know their *alter ego*. If you think you shoot like John Wayne or sing like Elvis or dribble a ball like Georgie Best, you'll most likely perform above your own standard.
- Before doing an MBA or any other important qualification, consider doing an MOFI first.

QUESTIONS

- What problem does your business solve?
- What good feelings does your business provide?
- When people meet you, do they leave feeling better or worse for the experience? The answer to this question will probably be the basis for most of your results in life.

POSTSCRIPT

Reilly was in 2nd Comm. when he heard a pompous lecturer espouse the importance of having a good academic qualification.

Afterwards, Reilly sauntered down town and queued up as he'd done a myriad of times before for a haircut with Tim.

Tim had recently announced his imminent retirement as a result of ill-health and both intuitively sensed that this might be their last haircut together.

When Tim bent down one last time to ask quietly which 'Star' Reilly would like to look like, Reilly held his arm firmly: "Tim. What exactly does N.H.Q.W. stand for?"

After a long and considered pause, Tim leaned down again and whispered quietly into Reilly's ear: "No Hairdressing Qualification Whatsoever."

Leaba i measc na naingeal agus na naoimh leat.

15

JUST CHECKING

A dissatisfied customer can tell up to 26 other people about their negative experience with you. Ignorance regarding your customers' perception of you is most certainly not bliss.

Declan O'Reilly, Empathy Marketing Group

It never ceases to amaze Reilly how the younger generation cannot imagine life without a mobile phone. Reilly is of a vintage that can recall vividly the lengths people had to go to make a simple phone call.

He remembers well working in his Mother's shop when a 14-year-old neighbour called Billy Brennan came in and says to Reilly: "Reilly, do you mind if I use the phone to make a quick call?"

Reilly knew Billy and his family and he knew that, although they'd been through hard times, they were the salt of the earth.

"Sure thing, Billy. Who's the lucky girl then?"

"Oh, this is strictly business, Reilly", as he picked up the phone and dialled.

Reilly wasn't listening *per se* but he couldn't help overhearing the conversation.

"Good morning. I just passed your house there and I couldn't help noticing your wonderful lawn and garden. It really is a credit to you. I wanted to tell you that I cut lawns to make some extra pocket money and I'm very neat at them. I also clip hedges. And I was wondering if ... ."

Billy seemed to pause for an eternity before continuing, "... I see. I understand. And tell me, are you satisfied with the work they are doing?"

Another long pause.

"That's fair enough. Well, would you mind if I called back again in a month or so?

"I can. Thank you very much. And once again, well done on maintaining such a lovely garden."

Billy hung up and replaced the receiver on the phone.

Reilly loved nothing more than a trier and was quick to intervene: "Billy, forgive me, but I happened to be standing near and I heard everything you said. I just want you to know that I'm a sales pro myself and everything you did on that phone was textbook. I want you to promise me you won't be disappointed because you didn't get that sale."

"Oh, Reilly, I got the sale all right. That was one of my customers. I was just checking up to see how I'm doing."

INSIGHTS

- Always be asking your customers how you're doing. Many times you'll be pleasantly surprised at the myriad ways your business makes a positive difference in people's lives. You need to know this. It gives you confidence.

- You also need to know when you're not doing a good job. Because when you find you've not been doing a good job, you can always fix it. You'd be amazed at how your customers will love you for this.

QUESTION

- When did you last ask your customers how you're doing?

16

YOU CAN'T DO BUSINESS SITTING ON YOUR ARMCHAIR

I wouldn't be advising anyone to provide good service.
Customers only ever remember two things when it comes to
service: really bad service and great service.
Good service is the norm; it is expected and will not create
any point of difference.
But providing great service will allow you to stand out.
And to provide great service, you need to ensure the culture
is right. Great service is delivered through motivated staff.
You can't instruct staff to provide great service.
It must be natural and it must be spontaneous.

Feargal Quinn

The first thing Reilly noticed about Feargal Quinn was a garish, bright green tie-pin, festooned with armchairs, above the letters YCDBSOYA.

"What's with the tie-pin, Feargal?", says Reilly curiously.

"When staff were promoted to store manager roles, I always made a point of presenting them with one of these tie-pins. The letters stand for 'You Can't Do Business Sitting On Your Armchair'. All a bit of fun but it still served to get a message across.

"The bottom line is that, as leaders and managers, you can't run a business from behind your desk. You have to make time to be on the front line, not always strategising or doing paperwork or surfing social media."

As if to demonstrate his point, he ushered Reilly towards one of the check-out tills, took off his jacket, and proceeded to pack customers' bags.

Reilly had been detailed to track Feargal for the day in his Superquinn shop in Kilkenny and to report back to the MBA class in UCG on the experience. He was flabbergasted to observe one of the busiest people in the country packing bags. Later, he questioned Feargal on the effectiveness of his time usage.

"Feargal, you own 20 shops. You're Chairman of An Post, a Senator, and own a myriad of other business interests. Could you not get other people to pack the bags?"

"Of course I could, Reilly. But packing bags is the most effective use of a leader's time. I get to engage and understand our customers. Likewise, with my own people. Understanding your customers and people are possibly the most important activities in business. Followed closely by visibility. Your customers love to see you. As do your 'A' players. They want to see you recognising them doing a great job.

"Remember Reilly, being in business is like being in a goldfish bowl. Everything you do is visible. I spend at least an hour of every day on the shop floor connecting with customers."

After an hour or so, Feargal donned his jacket and asked Reilly to accompany him on a tour of the shop. As they proceeded down the centre aisle, an audible shouting reached their ears: "Where's the manager? I want to see the manager now".

Reilly looked for a suitable means of escape, but Feargal made straight for the source of the commotion.

There was a lady, incandescent with rage, holding a half-eaten chicken up for the whole shop to see.

"I'm Feargal Quinn. I own this shop. How may I help you?"

"Help me! You may well ask!"

And as a crowd of nosy shoppers gathered around, she regaled them with "the most embarrassing evening of her life". She claimed she'd bought the chicken in Superquinn the day before, in advance of entertaining important friends and the chicken was gone off.

As she continued to vent steam, Feargal listened intently without saying a word, and it was then that Reilly saw the evidence. It was there in front of them. The lady had the chicken half-wrapped in the plastic packaging of a competitor's store where she'd actually purchased it.

Reilly knew he needed to act fast, but discreetly. Moving to stand directly behind the lady, he began to point towards the bag, while simultaneously waving with his other hand to get Feargal's attention. But it was in vain; Feargal didn't seem to see. And then to compound matters, Feargal addressed the entire audience: "Dear customers. What happened Mary last evening is absolutely shocking and I can only apologise profusely for the embarrassment she must have felt.

"Mary, I can't undo the trauma of last evening but what I want you to do right now is go down to the butchers' section and get whatever cut of meat you'd like. Then I'd like you to go to the wine section and get six bottles of your favourite wine."

And he went on and on, giving her more and more, and all the time Reilly was frantically trying to attract his attention.

The rumpus petered out and it was only then that Reilly got a chance to appraise Feargal on the situation. Reading Reilly's mind, Feargal explained: "Reilly, I know what you're thinking. I saw the wrapper from the other store. Maybe that lady did try to rip us off. The thing is that a certain percentage of the population will set out to do that anyway and the finest of security systems in the world won't prevent it.

"And maybe she made a genuine mistake. Maybe, in her state of mind, she thought she bought the chicken here.

"Either way, I wasn't going to embarrass anyone in front of another 20 onlooking customers."

And pointing to a small gold boomerang brooch on his suit lapel, he explained: "Our mission in Superquinn can be conveyed in the symbol of a boomerang. Our only job is to get the customer to come back. Now, let's meet the team."

And for the next 20 minutes, Feargal had a stand-up meeting (they take less time) with his team. The agenda for the meeting was the feedback he'd received from the customers he'd spoken to in the first hour.

INSIGHTS

- YCDBSOYA.
- Allocate time to spend engaging with your customers every day.
- Allocate time to spend with your team every day.
- Tackle problems head-on and solve them on the spot.
- Admit it and 'fess up when you're wrong. In fact, even when you're not wrong.
- Your purpose in business is to get the customer to return.

QUESTIONS

- How much time have you spent with customers today?
- How much time have you spent with your team today?
- How much focus have you spent getting your customers to come back to you?

POSTSCRIPT

In recent times, YCDBSOYA has become an acronym for yet another business success strategy: 'You Can Do Business Solely On Your Apple'.

Two hundred years ago, the 'Agricultural Revolution' required ownership of vast tracts of land, creating a massive barrier to business entry. This was followed by the 'Industrial Revolution', where you needed expensive machinery and labour and loads of capital to break into the game.

When Reilly's father opened his shop *Teach a Bhréidín* in 1936, he needed premises, loads of tweed, and money to pay wages before he had any chance of winning at the game of business.

Today, all you need to play and win at the game of business is an idea, an Internet connection, and an Apple iPhone.

17

THE ANATOMY OF A SALE

Show me a successful person and I'll show you a salesperson.

Richard Denny

G o out and buy yourself a decent pair of shoes and do not attempt to show up at the wedding tomorrow in those old pieces of cardboard."

Reilly knew his goose was cooked. When the Mother issued a *diktat*, she expected to be obeyed. He resolved to expedite the matter as quickly as possible.

His strategy was no different than any of the last three times he had bought shoes. He legged it into the large multiple department store on Shop Street, with the idea of getting out as fast as he could.

These shops are designed for the non-discerning impulsive buyer like Reilly. The shoes are seductively merchandised to induce maximum impact with minimum engagement.

He spied the shoes. Checked they were the same as the last ones he had. Checked the price. Everything was going swimmingly, except the size.

With shoe in hand, he located a lone sales assistant contemplating her nails behind a cash counter.

"Can I have these in a size 8, please?", he asked.

She flashed him a sympathetic smile that would not have been out of character at a funeral.

"If they're not on display, we don't have them", she said discompassionately, as she studied a finger nail that had a wonderful impression of the American flag on it.

"How did you manage to do that so neatly?", he asked in a *faux* sarcastic voice, referring to the Stars and the Stripes.

She brightened up perceptively.

"My sister did a course in nail painting last weekend and I'm her guinea pig. She has to try out 10 different designs to pass her exam. What do you think of the others?"

Needless to say, Reilly re-emerged on Shop Street as poorly shod as he'd entered it, but now with a rapidly-rising temper. In some recess of his mind, he recalled the parting words of his mother: "I saw a lovely pair of sensible brogues in Geraghty's window".

The Second Sale

Reilly was giving his frustration the full nine yards as he entered Geraghty's shop. He was mouthing loudly as he climbed the stairs to the shoe department on the first floor.

"The only reason I'm in here is that the Mother sent me. You're the dearest shoe shop in Galway."

Aidan Malone, known to anyone who grew up in Galway 50 years ago as Sid, intercepted Reilly's rant before he could infect any more of his staff or customers.

Feeling the lapel of Reilly's suit jacket, he matched his tone by exclaiming: "Reilly, that's a great suit. Where did you get it?"

Reilly admired Sid's effort at deflecting his toxicity, but was far too agitated to let him away with it.

"I got it in Hanley's Sale", he retorted, referring to one of Sid's key competitors and hoping he'd provoke a bit of banter.

"Yea, it's a great brand. We don't stock it but what I like about it is that it looks great, it's a lovely light weight for the summer and it won't crinkle in the car and that's important to you, Reilly, when you drive as much as you do."

Reilly would never admit it, but he was impressed.

"You say you want to buy a pair of shoes, and by the sound of you, you want them quick. What do you want the shoes for?"

"Ah, come on, Sid. What a stupid question! What does anyone want a pair of shoes for? I want them to keep the water out of my feet and to get the Mother off my back."

"Will you be wearing them mostly for work or leisure?"

"I have loads of shoes for leisure. I need them for a wedding tomorrow and then entirely for work."

"What's a typical day at work?"

"You know what I do, Sid. I'm either standing up giving training courses or selling training courses to clients."

"How many training courses would you give a year?"

"I did 150 last year."

"So, all in all, you could be in front of maybe 1,500 people a year."

"I've never thought of it like that, but probably more, as I would do about one big conference presentation a month."

"So, either way, a lot of people are going to see your shoes."

"I guess so."

"Tell me, Reilly, what makes a great training session?"

"Sid, what is this? An interview for a job?"

"Seriously. What makes you any different from all the other trainers out there?"

Reilly had to admit it, Sid had him thinking.

"I suppose, Sid, the difference between me and the others is energy. I like to leave my clients pumped up and ready to take action."

"So, Reilly, it's fierce important for you to have high energy levels yourself."

"You got it in one, Sid!"

"Before I show you some shoes, Reilly, do you mind me asking you where you have bought your shoes up to now?"

"No problem, Sid. I buy all my shoes across the road in that big department shop. The shoes look well, they're light and they're cheap. I hate buying shoes and you can be in and out of that place in a minute – that is, if they have the size."

"You're right. They look very trendy and everyone seems to be wearing them. How well do they wear?"

"I haven't thought about that but I always seem to be buying shoes, and as I've told you already, I hate it."

"Would those", pointing to Reilly's well-worn and scuffed shoes, "be the first pair you bought this year?"

"You must be joking. They must be the third pair I've bought. I barely get three months out of them."

"Now, Reilly, I know you don't like buying shoes. And I know you're not too keen on the shoes in the window yet. But the facts of the matter are that shoes are a very important component of your business, your image and your energy levels. Doesn't it make sense to spend a small bit of time making a good decision?"

There was no way of disputing that, so Reilly nodded in the affirmative to Sid's diagnosis. Moreover, he was now mildly excited and intrigued as to how a pair of shoes could improve his business image and his energy levels. "Bring it on, Sid!", he thought.

Reverently holding a shoe similar to one in the window, Sid proceeded to tell Reilly that the shoes he stocks are hand-crafted in Portugal by a cousin of his called John Evans.

"We are the only stockists in Galway and I inherited the account from Sonny Molloy in High Street when he retired. Now before I explain to you the features of these shoes, I want you to try them on first."

As he handed Reilly the shoe, Reilly instinctively flipped it over and gasped at seeing the price.

"€150 for a pair of shoes", he roared. "I've never paid anything near that for a pair of auld shoes."

"I know €150 sounds expensive, Reilly, but compared to what?"

"Compared to the shop across the road. I can get these shoes I've on for €70. Less than half the price."

"Reilly, I'm going to say three things to you now about price. One, you're not going to pay €150 for those shoes. I'll give you a bit of discount, as I always do. Two, I'm going to give you three reasons why these shoes will actually make you money as opposed to cost you money. Third, I want to park the price issue for a moment while you try them on."

Having tried them on, Sid had Reilly walk all about the shop and even go outside to look at them in the daylight. As Reilly walked, Sid asked his brother Denis what he thought of them. Sid's cousin Sharon was also asked her opinion. They all thought the shoes were great and that Reilly would be delighted with them.

"The first feature of these shoes", Sid explained to Reilly, "is that they're hand-stitched, which means that you'll stand out in any company. This is very important in your line of work where first impressions are very important. In fact, a recent survey amongst business people said that your shoes are the third thing looked at after your face and suit and that eight out of 10 business people scored poorly on their quality of shoe. Furthermore, a class pair of shoes will set off the rest of your attire to great effect. My grandfather used always say to invest well in the accessories – they make a bad suit look great and a good suit look terrific.

"Now think about that, Reilly. You stand in front of at least 1,500 people a year. That is 1,500 moments of truth in front of customers who may or may not buy you. Why not stack the odds in your favour by making a great first impression every one of those 1,500 times?

"How do they feel to wear?", Sid asked Reilly.

Reilly had to concede they were as light as a feather.

"Now that's the second reason why these shoes are such an invaluable investment for you. Think about it. You're standing on your feet, six to eight hours a day. Did you know that each of your feet have about 200,000 nerve endings that connect with every organ in your body? The quality of your shoes impact directly the quality of your energy and that is precisely what your business is. I have barmen and hairdressers come from all over the country to buy these shoes because they know they'll be less tired at the end of a long day standing.

"Finally, Reilly, as a business person yourself, you're interested in value for money. Now these shoes, as you can see, cost €150. As I said, that sounds expensive but consider how long these shoes will last you. The former Rector of the Pro-Cathedral wrote to me on his retirement to tell me that he'd bought a pair of these shoes 10 years earlier and that they were still as good as new. Even if you were only to get one year from them, they're far better value than what you're paying at the moment."

As Reilly was pondering his improved image, and his enhanced comfort and the great value he was getting, Sid delivered the ultimate *coup de grâce*: "I'm going to put them in a bag for you and I want you to take them home and see what your Mother thinks of them."

"Sid, I'm leaving them on me. Now, what discount are you giving me?"

INSIGHTS

- The anatomy of the sale as presented by our first specimen – the nail fancier – resembles closely that of the anatomy of an amoeba: one dimensional and simple in the extreme. Yet this approach to selling – order-taking – is by far and away the most prevalent approach to sales in our society. Over two-thirds (68%) of customers who cease doing business with you do so because of apathy, or indifference, on behalf of your sales personnel.

- Sid, on the other hand, demonstrates all the characteristics of the consultative salesperson – a real pro. He looks, talks, thinks, acts and sells like a pro. He understands intuitively that selling is an art, a science and ultimately a game that is governed by the laws of empathy, cause and effect and strict ground rules.

  o It is an art in that people buy people first, and your product or service second.

  o It is a science in that there is a definite structure and body of knowledge that, if followed, will generate predictable results time and time again.

- And like any seasoned pro, Sid plays the game to win. That is not to say that he always does. For him, competing and performing at his best are his motives. Crucially, he loves selling, and win or lose, he is invigorated by the sale. That is his *mojo*.

QUESTIONS

- Are you a salesperson? (By the way, even if I don't know you, the answer is "Yes".)
- If so, are you an amateur or a pro?

POSTSCRIPT

Aidan (Sid) Malone is a third-generation retailer. His grandfather, Michael Geraghty, opened Geraghty's in 1935. Since then, it has prospered as one of Galway's leading gents' outfitters. You can see why.

18

THE ULTIMATE
MARKETING
DISCIPLINE

Doing business without marketing is like winking at an attractive person across a darkened room. You know what you're doing but nobody else does.

Anon.

D on Colleran and Reilly are great buddies. Together, they cut their leadership teeth with Junior Chamber International and got up to up to all sorts of *divilment* and *divarsion* in the process.

It was during this time that Don developed and honed a marketing discipline that enabled him to grow a business that would become the envy of his industry and peers.

Reilly was intrigued by Don's business acumen and plagued him for the secret. Eventually, Don relented and told Reilly to come to his office at 3pm the following Friday. In return for sharing the secret, Reilly would need to bring a copy of that day's *Connacht Tribune* and a few freshly-baked chocolate croissants.

As Reilly arrived, Don instructed his assistant Debbie that neither he nor Reilly were to be disturbed for the following hour and to hold all calls.

Having scoffed the croissants and coffee, Don asked: "Reilly, what are the items of construction most used by every builder and carpenter?"

Building and carpentry were not Reilly's subject areas of expertise, so he muttered, "Hammers".

"No, Reilly", says Don. "It's 2 x 4s; or 4 x 4s; or 2 x 6s; or 2 x 8s.

"And in marketing and selling, I've discovered that the magic number is 4 x 4s."

Proceeding to a clean whiteboard on the wall of his office, Don sketched out four squares. In one square, he wrote TEXTS; in another, EMAILS; in the third, LETTERS; and in the last, PHONE.

"Each Friday, I discipline myself to send four texts; four emails; four personal letters; and make four phone calls.

"It doesn't sound like a lot – but that's 16 x 40 weeks (since joining SMACHT, I now take 12 weeks off each year), which is 640 proactive connections a year.

"I have carefully tracked the results of these connections and I've discovered that 50% of them result in business of one description of another over the course of the year. That's close to 300 business transactions for an investment of just one hour a week."

"That makes sense in theory, Don, but how much does it cost to generate the names and where do you find them?"

"It costs precisely €3 a week or €150 a year and it's called the *Connacht Tribune*. Let's get marketing."

Don opened up the local newspaper at page three, where there was a full photo feature on the recent Croí Ball. Don quickly circled four of the ladies on the page and proceeded to compose a text which read: "Looking radiant on today's *Connacht Tribune*. Stunning outfit. Have a great weekend. Don".

He cut and pasted the text and sent it to the four ladies.

"Time investment – four minutes", he says to Reilly forensically.

Don then flicked over some pages and went to the business section and quickly identified four businesses that had been in the news that week.

He scripted a short, positive and congratulatory email and proceeded to send it to each of those four recipients.

Already, his mobile phone began bleeping and he was able to show Reilly that two of the four ladies he'd texted had already come back to him, thanking him profusely for his kind words. One of them had requested a quote for an education policy for one of their kids.

"Of all the marketing media, the written word is now the most seductive", he explained to Reilly. "When was the last time you got a hand-written envelope in the post, Reilly?'"

Reilly couldn't remember.

"That's the point, Reilly. A hand-written envelope, written in blue fountain pen, addressed to you, is marketing gold. It's guaranteed to be opened every time."

And finally, Don identified another four people whom he called directly by phone. None of the four had even been aware that they'd been in the paper and were delighted to be told. Of the four, two made enquiries of a business nature and another said they'd be in contact the following week.

At 4pm on the dot, Don and Reilly departed the office for O'Connell's Pub across the Square, where Don explained that they would complete the final 2 x 2 of the working week.

"Right, Reilly, we will now enjoy two pints and connect with at least two people during each pint.

"Then we'll finish work and enjoy the weekend."

INSIGHTS

- Marketing and sales are less about flash, fancy websites and expensive advertising campaigns and ultimately about making the time and discipline to simply connect directly and personally with people.

- Marketing, therefore, is first and foremost a discipline. There is no substitute for connecting with people. Personally, regularly, sincerely and helpfully.
- Marketing and sales are key functions of every business and the success of your business is directly proportionate to the time you devote to them.
- Disciplines can be infinitely less punitive than they sound. By creating enjoyable and rewarding routines, you can create an incentive to want to perform your discipline. For Don, it's coffee, croissants, reading the local newspaper and imbibing a few pints.

QUESTIONS

- How long, and at what time, do you spend on focused marketing activity each week?

POSTSCRIPT

It sounds morbid, but it was anything but. On 3 July, 2020, Don saw Reilly's Mother's first year anniversary in the *Connacht Tribune* and rang him. They had a 40-minute chat, reminiscing on their auld relations who'd passed on. By the end of the call, Don had signed up to SMACHT and has continued to be a leading light ever since.

It just goes to show you that marketing cuts both ways!

ATTITUDE

19

WHO'S IN YOUR HOUSE?

The quality of your life depends on who's in your room.

Ivan Misner, Emery Stewart & Rick Sapio, *Who's In Your Room?*

A person's success in life can usually be measured by the number of uncomfortable conversations he or she is willing to have.

Tim Ferriss

They say you always remember your 'firsts': your first day at school; your first date; your first day in a new job. Although it's many years ago, Reilly will never forget his first business training gig.

He'd succeeded in getting 25 of the good and the great of Limerick's business community to attend a training course in the Ryan Ardhu Hotel on the Ennis Road in Limerick.

To say it was a career gamechanger was maybe over-egging it, but it sure felt like it at the time. Do a great job and profitable business would follow. Do anything less than a great job and it was "Good night, Irene".

As Feargal Quinn would remind him many years later, "Reilly, customers only ever remember two things: great service and bad service. There's no point being good".

Reilly was so apprehensive about the gig that he overnighted in the hotel in order that he'd be at his best.

He was wide awake early in the morning and rang his only direct relation at the time for a bit of moral support.

"What are you doing ringing me at this time of the night?', says his Mother, clearly annoyed. "I'm only just after falling asleep. This better be important."

"I'm ringing from a hotel in Limerick."

"What are you doing in Limerick?"

"I'm giving a course."

"You. Giving a course! To who?"

"Business people, Ma. Some of the most important and influential people in the Mid-West."

If she'd been half-sleep when he rang, she was fully awake now.

"What are you giving the course on?"

"Time management, Ma."

"You! Giving a talk on time management, of all things! Sure the dogs on our street know you'll be late for your own funeral. And have you seen the state of your bedroom? Hopefully, the course is a quick one?"

"The course is from 9am to 1pm."

"Four hours! Sure what'll you fill the time with? And what happens if you forget your lines? And what happens if they get up and walk out on you? Them important and influential business people are busy people and won't tolerate any old gibberish."

Reilly knew it was rude, but he put the phone down.

Strangely, his Mother's worst fears for him forced him to ask four questions he's been asking ever since when faced with scary situations:

- What am I worried about?
- What's the worst that can happen?
- Can I handle that?
- What can I do about it?

Worried about?

He was worried that the event mightn't go as well as he'd hoped and planned for.

Worst case scenario?

The worst that could happen was that his Mother's worst fears might be realised and that the audience might well get up and walk out.

Handle it?

He thought to himself that, even if this happened, nobody would die, and he'd learn from it and get back up and do one better somewhere else.

Do about it?

He remembered a time in his teenage years when his cousin and himself would be jumping off the cliffs in Rougey in Bundoran into the waves far below. They'd be terrified and ecstatic in equal measure. And as they'd be struggling with the decision to jump or not, his cousin would roar: "Reilly, hold your nose and jump".

And they always did.

And most of the times, they felt ecstatic afterwards.

And that's exactly what Reilly did.

And the workshop was a great success.

All the way from Limerick to Galway, Reilly dithered over his dilemma. He could choose to let the experience of that morning pass. Or he could choose to have an uncomfortable conversation.

He decided on the *módh díreach* (direct approach): "Ma, I'm never going to call you before a work gig again".

And, of course, unsurprisingly, she went ballistic: "Well, that's *galánta*, isn't it. My only son is never going to speak to me again".

And Reilly never, ever, ever did ring her prior to a gig that required his full focus and energy.

And equally, he never, ever, ever did a gig when he didn't call her afterwards. Whether the gig went swimmingly or belly-up, it didn't matter at that stage; they could have a chat without any drama.

Reilly has been telling that story publicly ever since and he always ends with the question: "Why did someone, as positive and caring as my Mother, have as negative an impact on her only child?"

People are generally kind and they say that she was worried about Reilly and that she was trying to protect him. Nonsense.

Although Reilly had been performing on stages since he was a nipper and had trained up as a time management coach, the reality was that Reilly's mother had never performed publicly in her life. To her, it was utterly outside of her comfort zone.

When she heard that Reilly would be performing in front of a group of 'important and influential business people' she instantly put herself in that situation and experienced immediate and extreme fear and terror.

Unfortunately, fear and terror can project as prolifically as a phone can connect two people speaking across the Atlantic.

You mightn't see them (the sound and fear waves) but you sure as Hell can feel them.

Someone else's fear can absolutely impact your performance.

INSIGHTS

- Sometimes, those closest to you, and who love you and care about you the most, can inadvertently have a negative impact on your energy levels.

- When you show up for important events, it behoves you to do so at your best. This requires astutely managing the energy level in 'your room'.

- The 'room' refers to a brilliant book called *Who's In Your Room?* In it, the authors encourage you to imagine your life as occurring in just one room. All the people you ever met are in that room. And they can't leave.

- Your strategy therefore is threefold. Firstly, there will be people in that room that you would profit from SEVERING your association with forever; these you will banish to the outermost corner of the room where they will be prevented from influencing you again. Secondly, there will be people, like Reilly's mother, that you will profit from LIMITING your association with, depending on the event you are showing up for at the time. Thirdly, there will be people you'd profit from EXPANDING your association with by bringing them closer to you in the room.
- Motivate yourself. Don't rely on others to do so. They may not be around, or in good form, when you really need them.
- Customers only ever remember two things: great service and bad service. Nobody remembers good service.
- Hold your nose and jump off a cliff at least once a day.

QUESTIONS

- Who will you banish to the corner of your room and thereby minimise their future impact on you?
- Who will you actively bring in and out of your room to match the situation that is currently playing out?
- Who will you bring closer to you in order to maximise their impact?

20

WHY SO MANY SUCCESSFUL PEOPLE ARE UNHAPPY

The meaning of life is to find your gift.
The purpose of life is to give it away.

Picasso

The two most important days in your life are the day you are
born and the day you find out why.

Mark Twain

Definiteness of purpose, combined with a positive mental
attitude, is the starting point of all worthwhile achievement.

Napoleon Hill

W hat d'ya learn in Harvard?"
Pádraig Ó Céidigh had just returned from attending a
month-long immersive leadership programme in Harvard and
Reilly was eager to learn some game-changers he could share with his
SMACHT community.

Back in the day, their routine would be a brisk walk out and back the
'Prom' in Galway, and then into Arabica restaurant for the breakfast.

Ó Céidigh peered out across Galway Bay, out towards the majestic
hills of Clare, and further out west to the Aran Islands where once he'd
flown thousands of people to experience the magic of Aran, and paused
for what seemed like an eternity.

"I learned why so many successful people I know are unhappy."

Reilly was rather hoping it might be less philosophical and a tad more
practical, but nonetheless elected to play the game.

"What is it?", Reilly asked.

"In a word, purpose. Purpose is key. That's my gift for you this
morning, Reilly."

Forever the consummate teacher, Ó Céidigh sensed Reilly didn't get it
and changed tack.

"Let me ask you, Reilly. How has your purpose changed over the past
two years?"

It was quintessential *múinteoir* (teacher) Ó Céidigh. Socratic learning.
Ask questions and listen.

'Well, I'm planning to build a business with more of an online
component so that if I ever get sick again I'll have something to fall back
upon."

"That's not a purpose", said Ó Céidigh, despairingly. "That's a goal.
And there's a world of difference between your purpose and your goals.

"Your purpose is what you exist for. Your purpose is what contributes
to your state of being now. Your purpose is what drives you when your
world is crumbling all around you. Your purpose is what energises you
when you should be exhausted. Your purpose is your journey.

"A-N-D", he said emphatically. "The worst thing you can ever do is
keep fulfilling a purpose that doesn't exist. That's what leaves countless
millions unfulfilled and unhappy and unchallenged."

"Sounds mighty", interjects Reilly. "But what does all that mean in
layperson's language?"

"Let's have the breakfast, Reilly. It might become clearer then'"

Over breakfast, Pádraig explained to Reilly that the entire Harvard experience could be summarised in the following story from Steve Jobs.

As a young student, Jobs elected to drop out of his mainstream science degree to pursue a course in calligraphy. There appeared to be no rhyme nor reason for doing this course other than that he was fascinated by the different fonts and how they presented to the reader. Some 10 short years later, that course would become the inspiration and the basis for every modern digital typeface that you see today.

Jobs would later say of the experience: "You can't connect the dots looking forward; you can only connect them looking backwards. So you have to trust that the dots will somehow connect in your future. You have to trust in something – your gut, destiny, life, karma, whatever. This approach has never let me down, and it has made all the difference in my life".

"Reilly, trust that you too will someday connect the dots."

It would be another week before Reilly connected the dots. He was MC at a function to celebrate the fifth anniversary of BioInnovate – a dynamic venture between NUIG and Stanford University, which combines resources to catalyse and lead medical innovation.

Over dinner, he sat beside Doctor Faisal Sharif, the clinical director of the programme, and an eminent cardiologist with an outstanding reputation for competency and care in the west of Ireland.

He'd been regaling Reilly with a typical day in his life.

"I was on call last night and spent most of the night successfully resuscitating a young man who was very ill. Today, I had a long list for surgery. I also had a board meeting with one of the most exciting medical devices businesses in Ireland this evening. And now I get to address this audience of the good and great of the medical devices industry in Ireland here."

"Why do you do it?", said Reilly, intrigued at the sheer level of intensity that Faisal lives his life at.

"Reilly, at my first lecture to every new group of students, I share the following thoughts with them:

"If you want to be happy for an hour, eat a steak.
"If you want to be happy for a day, play golf.
"If you want to be happy for a week, go on a cruise.
"If you want to be happy for a month, get a car.
"If you want to be happy for a year, get a house.
"If you want to be happy forever, serve humanity.

"I am privileged to serve humanity."

The dots connected instantly for Reilly.

Faisal was living on purpose.

Purpose first. Goals second.

INSIGHTS

- It's futile, if not downright destructive, to have a goal that runs contrary to your purpose.
- Your primary purpose, therefore, in life is to unearth your purpose. When you live congruently with your purpose, you unleash your natural genius.
- Trust you'll connect the dots.
- 'Serving humanity' mightn't be the worst place to begin your search.

QUESTION

- What is your purpose?

21

IQ IS GREATLY OVER-RATED

You are the average of the five people you are surrounded by most of the time.

Jim Rohn

Reilly was thrilled to bits when he made the cut to be accepted for boarding school in Roscrea in 1972. Eighty boys sat the entrance exam. Reilly came 52nd. The school accepted 55.

On the morning of the first day, classes were allocated for each boy on the big notice board outside the Refectory: 20 were assigned to 2A; 20 to 2B; and 15 to 2C.

As Reilly made his way to 2C, he felt for maybe the first time in his life what it feels like to be behind in the queue. He resolved, however, to park that for the meantime and get on with life in 2C.

So when one of his new class mates proclaimed that they were that part of the class that made the first part possible, he cheerfully joined in the *craic*.

He continued to do so until the following Sunday, when his Mother arrived to review progress.

She was incandescent when she learned he was in the C class and demanded to know why.

"IQ", says Reilly calmly. "Classes are allocated, for better or worse, on the basis of IQ as tested by the entrance examination and I rate 52 out of 55 on that scale. I'm there on merit. I have a low IQ and I might as well accept that for what it is."

"We'll soon see about that", says Mother, beating a march towards the Dean of Studies' office, with Reilly in her wake.

Reilly's Mother stood a statuesque 5' 11" in her bare feet and Fr. Emmanuel, the Dean of Studies, a tidy 5' 5" with shoes on.

She now extended her height to the maximum that her high heels would allow and addressed the Dean squarely in the eye: "I want Reilly out of the C class immediately. His Father is dead and, if anything happens to me, he'll need a job to support himself. What chance has he of ever getting a job if he's in the C class?"

The Dean, to his credit, remained unfazed: "Mrs. Reilly, in terms of future employment opportunities, I must reassure you that Reilly couldn't be in a better position. In my not inconsiderable experience as a Dean of Studies, I have found that those in the C class invariably end up giving jobs to those in the A class".

Reilly felt hugely uplifted by this validation of his possible future potential, but his Mother wasn't wearing one bit of it.

"In order to get on in life, Reilly, you need standards. And right now, I have heels that are higher than your standards. You need to raise your standards higher. I don't care how you change that IQ of yours but, by the next time, I come to visit, I want you in the B class."

And he was.

But his ascension to the B class, and later to the top of the A class, had little to do with IQ.

It had much more to do with a combination of getting around the right people and finding something he loved to do.

Reilly discovered that there were trials for an Irish debating team being held one particular afternoon by a teacher called Brendán O'Rourke. Brendán, it seemed, was eager to put Irish debating in Roscrea on the same standing as English debating, in which the school was one of the best in Ireland at that time.

A former All Ireland winning sprinter and Kerry footballer himself, he was a competitor by nature, and his mission was to build a dream Irish debating team that would be the first non-Gaeltacht school to win the Gael Linn Munster debating championship.

Reilly already had good Irish and was a decent storyteller and actor.

But Brendán saw things in Reilly he never saw in himself. Crucially, he saw in Reilly traits that would complement those traits he saw in other members of the team he was building.

By 1978, the dream team was coming together. A generational wonder-kid called Kieran Fitzgerald had emerged as probably the greatest debating talent that had ever entered the hallowed halls of Roscrea College. A sixth year called Brian Cowen had a reputation for eviscerating the arguments of the opposition. And, in the middle, was Reilly who loved to tell stories.

In 1979, Roscrea was the first non-Gaeltacht team to win the Gael Linn Munster championship when they beat Dingle's finest at a neutral venue in Limerick. It would be a poignant victory for Brendán, because there's a part of every Kerry person that lives to win.

INSIGHTS

- Reilly had the same IQ when he sat his entrance examination as he did when he sat his Leaving Certificate, where he got nearly maximum points in Irish and English. The difference was the teachers, his peers, and the standards.

- By far and away the biggest influence on your destiny is the peer group you're most influenced by.

- At the core of this centre of influence are teachers. They probably are the single greatest influence on your destiny and those of your family. Make it your business to get around great teachers.

- Great teachers and great leaders see things in other people they don't see in themselves.

QUESTIONS

- Who do you need to sever your association with?
- Who do you need to limit your association with?
- Who do you need to expand your association with?

POSTSCRIPT

That little Irish debating group went its separate ways after Roscrea.

It surprised nobody when Fitz became a newsreader on RTÉ's main news programme, shortly after leaving school. Brian Cowen went on to become Taoiseach of Ireland at the lowest point of our economic development. Reilly continues to tell stories with morals.

As for Brendán, this being early March, he has been live on Radio na Gaeltachta every day this week at 12:10, providing tips for Cheltenham.

No doubt, he will also speak on air with another of his students from that time, who this week became the first trainer ever to win 100 races in Cheltenham.

Brendán O'Rourke's three passions are teaching, the Irish language and horses. Isn't it a wonderful success to be able to say that, in his mid-80s, he is still doing all three live on radio?

He revealed his secret of success to Reilly many years ago: "*Ni bhíonn an rath ach mara mbíonn an smacht.* (There's no success without discipline.)"

22

HOW HEAVY ARE YOUR WORRIES?

I realise there's something incredibly honest about trees in winter, how they're experts at letting go.

Jeffrey McDaniel

R eilly and Mrs. Reilly snuck into Tully's Pub in Kinvara for one quick one, *en route* home from Dublin last Saturday. They'd no sooner sat on two stools in the old shop part of the pub when David Noone presented Reilly with the most beautiful creamy pint of fresh porter straight into his hand.

"It's all yours, Reilly, if you can tell me exactly how heavy that pint of porter is. I'll be back in a minute to hear your answer. If you get it right, the pint's all yours. If not, I'll give it to someone else."

Reilly cradled the glass reverently in his hand and gave the question the respect it called out for.

David is an expert on all matters relating to weights and measures. He's also a stickler for accuracy and precision. The thing was, Reilly wouldn't know the weight of a fluid ounce from a fluid ovulation. He certainly hadn't a clue how heavy the pint was.

But he was ever the competitor and the allure of that beautiful pint was exercising all his wit. It's in moments of high-intensity focus like these that our true creativity for solving problems is unleashed and activated.

Whispering quietly to Mrs. Reilly, he says: "Pretend you're checking the lotto numbers, but google instead how heavy a pint of porter is, and scribble the answer down discreetly on the beer mat".

When David returned, Reilly feigned humility and declared without the least trace of triumphalism: "That pint weighs 16 Imperial ounces or, more specifically, 19.2152 fluid ounces".

As Reilly raised the glass towards his lips, David put a firm and restraining hand on his wrist and said: "Not yet, Reilly. That wasn't the question I asked you. I didn't ask you the weight of the pint. I asked you how heavy it is. I'll be back in another minute to hear your answer".

By the time David returned, Reilly's hand had begun to physically tremble and shake.

"Well, Reilly, how heavy is the pint now?"

"A lot heavier than it was a minute ago", said Reilly tetchily. "And it's getting heavier and heavier by the minute, so will you cut to the chase with your psycho-play and tell me the answer. Let me either drink the pint or put it down."

"That's the answer in a nutshell, Reilly. The answer is how long you decide to hold the glass.

"When you think about it, it was no problem to hold that glass for a minute. But after two or three minutes, it began to become a bit uncomfortable. If you held it for an hour, you could end up paralysed.

"The point is the weight of the glass never changes. It's constant. The key issue is how long you choose to hold on to it. Does that make sense?"

Reilly did something he hadn't done since being a first year student in College Week. He drained that entire pint down in one glorious gulp.

"It makes perfect sense, David."

INSIGHTS

- Life is a lot like Reilly holding onto that pint in the bar in Tully's. We can handle most things in life – even the big challenges – for short periods of time. However, if we hold on to them for a while, they become uncomfortable. If we continue to hold onto them, even the most trivial of worries could paralyse you.

- The solution is to stop holding on to them and put them down.

QUESTION

- What worries and stresses and cares can you put down now?

23

LIVE LIFE LIKE A BUFFALO

The impediment to action advances action.
What stands in the way becomes the way.

Marcus Aurelius

Reilly's Uncle Stiofáin was an avid traveller. Each year, he'd visit his brother in America and together they'd explore the vast plains and mountains of that massive nation. And on his return, he'd fill Reilly up with tales and stories of that great land.

This particular year, they'd been to Colorado and he was explaining to Reilly that it is one of the few places in the world where cattle and buffalo roam together. He described to Reilly the similarities between these two animals and yet how one is much more intelligent than the other.

"When a storm approaches, both animals can sense it in their being but are programmed to respond to it differently. The cattle, knowing that the prevailing winds come from the west, instinctively head east, in order to outrun the storm. But as you know, cattle are slow and awkward and are rapidly overhauled by the speed of the storm. And instead of actually outrunning the storm, they simply end up running with it.

"The buffalo, on the other hand, resolutely wait until the storm is at its height, and then proceed to charge head-on in to it. To be sure, it's difficult and frightening to begin with, but very quickly they emerge on the far side of the storm. Thus they sensibly end up minimising their exposure to it.

"And so it is with people. Many flee their problems, hoping to avoid the pain and suffering involved in confronting them. In so doing, ironically they maximise their exposure to misery and hardship.

"Clever people, however, realise that problems are part and parcel of life, and that the quicker and harder they charge at them, the quicker they are resolved and overcome.

"Reilly, you may think a time will come when all is rosy and you'll be problem-free. The reality is that you'll always have problems. And while this sounds negative, it doesn't have to be.

"The day you realise that, by charging head-on at your greatest challenges, is the day you become free, because that's the day you realise you have the solution to overcoming your cares and worries."

INSIGHTS

- Life is a series of problems. We have a choice: we can hope they solve themselves or we can choose to proactively solve them. One is a cattle mentality; the other is a buffalo mindset.

- One of the great disciplines in life is delaying gratification. Delaying gratification is a process of scheduling the pain and pleasure of life in such a way as to enhance the pleasure by meeting and experiencing the pain first and getting it over with. According to M. Scott Peck in the book *The Road Less Travelled*, 'It is the only decent way to live'.
- Think of it this way. Many people begin their working day by putting off or procrastinating on activities they know they should do but don't like doing. They then proceed to worry and stress about those procrastinations right throughout the day. Wouldn't it be preferable to get them over with early in the day?
- Mark Twain had a metaphor for getting hard things done: if you have to eat a live frog, do it right away and everything after that will be easier by comparison. 'Eat that frog' is a great metaphor for life.
- The obstacle is the way.

QUESTIONS

- What areas in your life would benefit from a buffalo mentality?
- What frogs will you eat this week?

24

IRISH LOBSTERS

Feel the fear and do it anyway.

Susan Jeffers

There was no doubting the caller. The caller ID couldn't be clearer: "Bank. Business Branch".

Reilly considered ignoring it and letting it go straight into his voice mail but he knew they'd persist until they got him. And he'd discovered that facing the music head-on was always the best strategy in dealing with the banks. He thought his account was in order, but you just never knew with the bank.

"Reilly speaking", he faked, in a mock cheerful tone.

"Reilly, we're in a bit of a pickle and we're counting on you to bail us out."

Bailing the bank out of pickles was a position Reilly was wholly unaccustomed to and compelled him to seek urgent clarity.

"Now, let me get this straight. You, the bank, are ringing me and you want me to bail you out. Are you sure it's me, Reilly, you're looking for, and not Jean-Claude Trichet from the European Central Bank?"

"It's you, Reilly. We need a *currach*. Today. And we need someone to take our man out in the *currach*. Our area of expertise includes corporate financing and regrettably does not extend to *currach*ing. And someone in head office said that you'd be our man. And bear in mind that it won't be forgotten if you rescue us. You get my drift!"

There was no better man than Reilly when it came to drifting, so he simply said, "What's the story?"

"Our client is an international industrialist of considerable means and intends investing in a substantial medical devices business in either Galway or Glasgow. We are most eager that he should commit to Galway, which would be of significant value to our portfolio.

"As such, we are pulling out all the stops in an effort to win him over. The Board of the Bank had intended bringing him to Ashford Castle this evening for dinner, but an unforeseen difficulty has just arisen.

"On the flight from New York, our client saw an in-flight video featuring the use of traditional Irish *currach*s on Galway Bay. It seems to have triggered some inexplicable emotional urge in him to go out on such a craft and nobody in the bank knows anyone with a *currach*. Hence, Reilly, I can't emphasise how impressed the Board of the Bank would be if you could accompany our client on a *currach* today."

"Have your man waiting outside the Branch at 4pm, and tell him to bring his wellies."

Reilly spotted him immediately. Surrounded by a cohort of pinstripe-suited bankers, there stood this enormous man with a new pair of shining wellingtons. Reilly estimated that if he was one stone in weight, he was at least 25.

Reilly quickly threw the empty Supermac's bag from the front seat of the car and brushed off the dog hairs, just as half of the business branch escorted their man into the seat.

"The name's Alphonsus Callinan, but my buddies call me Phonsie."

Reilly and Phonsie got along like the proverbial house on fire. They discussed fishing, shooting, drinking and other matters of universal importance and, in no time at all, they arrived at the slipway in New Quay, County Clare.

Reilly's man, the legendary Gerry Sweeney, had his *currach* all rigged up and ready to rock. Reilly introduced the pair and said he'd await them in Linnane's Lobster Bar upon their return.

"Come here, Reilly. You're coming with us", said Gerry, assertively.

"What for, Gerry?", says Reilly.

Gerry was never one to use two words when one would do and simply said: "Ballast".

"Understood", said Reilly and Phonsie in unison, and so commenced a most enjoyable and balanced afternoon's angling on Galway Bay. Gerry and Reilly occupied the stern end of the *currach* and Phonsie happily countered their combined weight, and that of the engine, in the bow.

Gerry is one of the most accomplished lobster fishermen in Ireland and the catch that day didn't disappoint. In almost every second lobster pot was a lobster. Gerry would expertly extricate the lobster live, throw it into a *cisean* or basket in the centre of the *currach*, and then re-bait the pot.

Things were going swimmingly for a period. Phonsie was beside himself with chat. It was as if his entire inner child had been released and rejuvenated.

But then gradually, Phonsie became quieter and more subdued.

And then he asked what Reilly considered a very valid question.

Feeling the delicate tarred canvas of the *currach* with his fingers, and eyeing the ever-increasing mound of writhing live lobsters attempting to summit the rim of the basket, Phonsie quietly said: "Gerry, what would happen if one of them lobsters ever escaped from the basket?"

Gerry gave the question the thought it deserved and philosophically replied: "You haven't a thing in the world to be afraid of, Phonsie, because them are Irish lobsters. And anytime anyone of them lads gets to the top, the rest of them drag him back down".

Reilly sensed the business was going to Galway.

INSIGHTS

- The 'Irish lobster' is a metaphor for those people who actively seek to pull you down – particularly when you are beginning to make progress in the world. This hindrance can be physically, but more often than not mentally, emotionally and psychologically.
- The strategy is simply to be aware of their existence and to sever your association with them.
- Never underestimate the amount of business done in a boat or a golf course or out for a walk in a beautiful setting. Look for opportunities to entertain your best clients in stimulating settings.
- Answer those calls that fill you with fear. Simply feel the fear and do it anyway, as Susan Jeffers so memorably advised.

QUESTION

- Who are the 'Irish lobsters' in your business and life?

25

WINNING IS NOT EVERYTHING

... the important thing in life is not to triumph but to compete ... not victory but combat ... not to have vanquished but to have fought well ... not winning but taking part ...

Pierre de Coubertin, founder of the modern Olympic Games

R eilly knew Joe Young long before he ever knew that Joe was a superstar. That's the thing about superstars. They don't carry calling cards. They don't need to.

Reilly's Uncle Paddy and Joe were lifelong friends, and once or twice a year, they'd take Reilly off with them snipe-shooting to the family place in Carrantrila, outside Dunmore in County Galway.

The first part of the day was run with military precision. Under strict orders from Reilly's Mother, he was assigned to march beside Joe because Joe was regarded as the epitome of safety and reliability.

Together, they'd march at a brisk pace between the fronds of heather of the Móinteach and Annach bogs. Sometimes, the heather was taller than Reilly but Joe, shotgun broken in one arm, would cheerfully haul Reilly up before he was swallowed by the bog.

What Reilly didn't appreciate at that age was that snipe are by and far away the most difficult game bird to shoot in these islands. Few marksmen ever shoot many snipe.

Joe bagged two in his first two shots. He called it a day at an even dozen, not having missed a single shot.

By the time they'd completed their march of the bogs, word had spread like a furze fire in August that Joe Young was on the bog and so a sizeable cohort of Carrantrila's finest had assembled at the back gate of Coen's Avenue.

In a parish that had supplied the Donnellan brothers, the Keenan brothers, Jack Mahon and Séamus Leyden to the four All Ireland winning sides of '56, '64, '65, and '66, they knew their football in Carrantrila. They didn't call them 'The Slashers' for nothing.

After inspecting the bag of game, Reilly was devastated that nobody commented on the excellent marksmanship. These men were not easily impressed.

And, inexorably, the topic *du jour* turned to football. Although Joe had lined out for Galway in three All Ireland hurling finals, the small ball didn't particularly excite or impress these men. They were singularly footballing men.

They began with the '66 final in which their neighbour, Johneen Donnellan, had captained the side with his brother Pateen playing at midfield. Their father Mick, also an All Ireland winner in 1925, sadly died at the match.

But it was the 1956 final that roused these stoic men to life.

Described by many as the greatest football match of that, or any other era, Joe had lined out at corner forward beside Sean Purcell and Frank Stockwell – 'The Terrible Twins' from Tuam.

And whilst Stockwell scored 2-5 from play that day – a record that was never equalled in a 60-minute final – and Purcell went on to be acclaimed as one of the immortal Princes of the game, it was Joe Young whom the Carrantrila men revered the most.

"Stocky and the Master nailed them that day, but if they did itself, it was you that put it on a plate for them, Joeen. Galway'd never have beaten that Cork side without you that day."

Joe shrugged it off like water off a duck's back, preferring instead to focus attention on others and away from himself.

What Reilly discovered in the car on the way home was that Joe had actually sustained a fractured collar bone early in that game but continued to play on irrespective and to push through the pain barrier. Joe never told anyone during the game and rarely spoke about it afterwards.

Thirteen years later, whilst serving with the UN in Israel, he sustained an infinitely more sinister injury. Responding to a call to help another soldier in trouble, he triggered a land mine that destroyed his UN vehicle and killed a fellow military observer. To compound matters, it was not possible to airlift him to hospital until nightfall to avoid Israeli shooting.

When miraculously, he regained consciousness, a doctor confided to him: "You should be dead. You've been given an improbable second chance today".

Joe's cheerful response was: "In that case, I get to celebrate two birthdays from now on".

Like the fractured collar bone in the final of '56, Joe never discussed the land mine explosion, preferring to dismiss it instead as 'the accident'.

At Joe's funeral in Barna, his daughter Orla delivered a wonderful eulogy in which she shared the mantra, and legacy, that she and her sisters had been brought up with by Joe:

For when the Great Scorer comes
To write beside your name.
He'll ask not if you won nor lost,
But how you played the game.

INSIGHTS

- Joe Young, first and foremost, practiced service. Whether on the playing field or the battle field or a bog showing care to a young child, his first instinct was always to serve others. And never more so than when his own life was at stake.

- Winning is not always all that it's cracked up to be. You can't always legislate for victory. What you can always control, however, is how you play the game of life.

- Champions are not removed from pain. They suffer it too, but play through it regardless and do so with a smile and good cheer. They refuse to complain or whinge but get on with it notwithstanding.

- Joe Young was a man you could take to the bog, or to a match, or to war.

QUESTIONS

- How are you playing the game of life?
- What will your legacy be?

26

YOU DON'T *HAVE* TO
DO ANYTHING

'Getting' to do something is the true blessing in life.
Gerry Duffy

R eilly found himself in 'have-to' land during the week.
- Have to finish the proposal for ...
- Have to start getting clients for the next SMACHT.
- Have to get 52 stories to the publisher by ... .
- Have to surprise Mrs. Reilly, for no reason at all.
- Have to attend the annual appointment with the cardiologist on Friday.

Things finally came to a head at the cardiology appointment when the cardiologist suggested he wear a heart monitor for 72 hours to check for any untoward rhythms.

"Ah, do I really have to?", says Reilly, thinking about the upcoming weekend and the discomfort of having this odious thing strapped to his chest.

Reilly and the cardiologist go back a long way. She has his number and is well wise to his aversion to all forms of medical intervention.

"Actually, Reilly, you don't have to. You get to."

"What are you talking about, Doc", says Reilly suspiciously.

"Two people sat in this surgery earlier today. They buried their son last month, who died from a heart attack. Like you, he won't have to wear a heart monitor either.

"Unlike him, you get to."

Reilly repaired with alacrity and a fully-charged heart monitor to Linnane's for his Friday TTPs (tea-time pints).

As he reflected on the advice of his doctor, he was reminded of another life-changing conversation he'd had with the legendary Gerry Duffy in the Mullingar Park Hotel back in February.

In 2010, inspired by looking at a photograph of an overweight version of himself, Gerry resolved to run 32 marathons in 32 days. A year later, he completed the inaugural UK DECA-Iron Distance Triathlon, an event dubbed 'the toughest 10-day endurance challenge in the world'. His book chronicling the experience, *Tick, Tock, Ten*, is a cracking read and was shortlisted for Irish Sports Book of the Year.

Gerry is now a full-time professional speaker and is outstanding in that field. Reilly asked him straight up how he went from being an overweight and mediocre person to elite athlete and national authority on goal-setting.

"I became aware of a language I was speaking. Frequently, I'd catch myself saying things like, 'I have to swim 100 lengths in the pool tomorrow' or 'I have to run 20 miles this weekend'.

"One day, the penny dropped that I don't *have* to run or I don't *have* to swim or I don't *have* to cycle. I don't even *have to* take on sporting ambitions, such as running consecutive marathons, or attempting ultra-distance triathlons either. I don't *have* to do any of it.

"I became aware that I was blessed to *get* the opportunity to do these things. Not only do I *get* to compete in sports, I now *get* to work in it, I *get* to run my own business, I *get* to give talks, *get* to meet deadlines, *get* to source new clients, *get* to write, *get* to speak, *get* to travel ...

"Before this epiphany, my mindset told me that I *had* to do it all. Now I realise I don't. *I get to.*

"One simple word changed in a sentence, transformed my life."

INSIGHTS

- You don't *have* to do anything. You *get* to.

QUESTIONS

- What do you get to do today?
- Does that feel better than having to?

27

THE ULTIMATE WORRY FORMULA

Do the thing you fear and the death of fear is certain.

Ralph Waldo Emerson

R eilly, I need you to call me", was all it said on the voice message. A fairly innocuous message if it had come from your mother or Flaherty or even your bank manager. Ominous in the extreme however, when it was from your cardiologist.

He replayed the message, hoping he might have gotten it wrong.

"Reilly, I need you to call me."

He dithered. Then decided to listen to the message again.

There was no doubting the tonality in that voice. There was kindness there, and caring too. There was also a distinct "don't mess me about" there too.

From some recess of his mind came the whisper, "D.I.N. – Do It Now".

He dialled the number, and willed for all he was worth that she was anywhere but at her phone.

Same voice. Same tonality. Different words.

"Reilly, you didn't score an A in your cardiac MRI."

On a different day, in a different context, he'd have loved that headline.

But, in the few moments it had taken her to utter those words, his life seemed to stutter and stall and sway in suspense.

It was subtle as a brick – saying nothing, yet saying everything.

"What's the story?"

"The MRI has detected a nodule or mass on your right atrium. I've contacted the Blackrock Clinic. They're the 'go to' people on this and they'll see you at 8am on Friday."

"Hang on a second", he said, with some assertiveness. "I'm giving a training course on Friday."

She paused for what seemed an eternity.

"I'll be there", he said compliantly.

For more years than he could care to remember, Reilly had been helping his clients solve big worries with a process he had named 'The Ultimate Worry Formula'.

It occurred to him with a smidgen of irony that now was as good a time as any to test the effectiveness of the formula – on himself.

On his notepad, he scribbled the first of the six questions in the formula:

What are you worried about?

"I'm scared stiff that I'm going to die."

What are the facts?

"An MRI has detected a growth somewhere in my heart."

What's the worst that can happen?

"I could die."

Can you accept that?

"With great difficulty. But if I have to, I have to. Everyone has to go sometime."

What can you do about it?

"I can:

- Refuse to worry about it until I get the full facts on Friday, because worrying solves nothing.
- Show up in that hospital on Friday as the best patient I can possibly be.
- Insist on only meeting with totally positive people over the next few days and actively avoid all negative people and influences.
- Surrender this entire journey into the hands of a Higher Power. In fact, I can thank the Higher Power in advance for a successful outcome.
- Stay off alcohol until this is through, because drink only compounds negative feelings and, right now, I need to be at my mental and emotional best.
- Stay busy all the time and refuse to allow myself for even a second to feel sorry for myself.

And speaking of which, I can now go for a run out the Prom and look out over Galway Bay."

What will you do about it?

He slipped on his tracksuit and runners and jogged out along the Prom.

And although the facts remained the same, he felt better and more in control on his return.

INSIGHTS

- Like it or like not, life is a series of problems that cause worry. You can either choose to ignore them or deal with them. The following questions are a structured way of confronting life's problems and worries:

- o *What are you worried about?* Our Mothers had some sage advice when they said, "A problem shared is a problem halved". Sharing a problem helps identify it; clarify it; and solve it. Remember that problems buried alive in your mind never die.
- o *What are the facts?* Refuse to waste a moment worrying until you have established the precise facts behind what you're worried about. Many of the things we worry unnecessarily about never happen.
- o *What's the worst case scenario?* There's a certain release about facing up to the very worst outcome.
- o *Can you handle the worst if it happens?* This is another great question, because the greatest fear of all is not the actual event itself but whether you can handle that event.
- o *What* can *you do about it?* This question appeals to the creative problem-solving part of your brain – the prefrontal cortex. The thing is that, in order for it to work, the amygdala has to be quietened first. That's the purpose of the first four questions.
- o *What* will *you do about it?* This is your plan of action.
- Surrender your worry and plan of action to a Higher Power. One of the most effective forms of prayer is not a prayer of supplication but rather to be thankful in advance for a successful outcome.

QUESTIONS

The power in these questions is best unleashed when you physically write out your answers. Don't be tempted to answer these questions in your head.

- What am I worried about?
- What are the facts behind what's worrying me?
- What's the worst case scenario?
- Can I accept and handle it if it happens?
- What *can* I do about it?
- What *will* I do about it?

CASH

28

STOP THINKING LIKE
AN ACCOUNTANT

---

*If there is one thing that will forever change your
relationship with money, it is the understanding of
'Parkinson's Law'. You need to intentionally make less
money available to operate your business. When there is
less, you will automatically run your business more
frugally and more innovatively.*

**Mike Michalowicz, *Profit First: A Simple System to Transform Any
Business from a Cash-Eating Monster to a Money-Making Machine***

Profit is not an event. It's a habit.

Mike Michalowicz

After more than 40 years, Reilly can still hear the screech of the chalk on the blackboard. Vinny Leahy, Roscrea's resident Commerce teacher, was explaining the First GAPP (Generally Accepted Accounting Principle):

SALES - EXPENSES = PROFIT

Reilly would continue to hear that formula trotted out throughout his B. Comm. degree in UCG and then again in almost every other business he worked in thereafter.

Logically, it made perfect sense.

Sell like the clappers; spend as little as possible; and pocket the difference.

Reilly figured on bringing the formula all the way to the bank.

He was good at selling and, in his first year in business, he delivered eight national training programmes for the newly-formed County Enterprise Boards.

He resolved to pay himself little more than basic expenses until the business got airborne and profitable.

He can still remember the day he visited the accountant to determine whether he had made a profit. He had felt confident about the outcome and insisted on bringing Mrs. Reilly along with him to celebrate the result.

There was much tapping on computers and some frantic whirring of printers before the accountant administered a series of swirls and twirls with his Montblanc Meisterstück pen before declaring: "Well done. You made a profit of €17,000. Not to be sniffed at in your first year in business".

Reilly was just beginning to feel the first surge of pride, before it was swiftly stifled by Mrs. Reilly.

"A profit of €17,000", she hissed frostily. "Where's the money in the bank then?"

There was the Mother of a silence before the accountant explained testily: "You must understand that this is accounting profit, which is anything but synonymous with money in the bank".

Mrs. Reilly wasn't for holding back.

"So what you're telling me is that we made a profit – even though there's *nada* in the bank."

Pleased that his efforts at elucidation were being understood, the accountant fatally replied: "Precisely!"

"I'd sooner attend a gynaecologist than ever have to visit an accountant again", says Mrs. Reilly frostily as she exited the accountant's office for her first – and final – time.

As there were few pleasantries exchanged on their homeward journey, Reilly had ample time to rethink his approach to generally accepted accounting principles.

Below is what he concluded.

INSIGHTS

- Accountants view profit differently to business people. They regard profit primarily as a figure to be calculated to determine taxable income for the Revenue.

- Business people see profit as money in the bank.

- Reilly resolved that, from that day on, money in the bank would be his primary business objective. So, he agreed a number that would be in the bank at a specific date and worked back.

- He set up a simple system where all revenue was channelled into a central holding account. From that, he set up four separate accounts into which a percentage of all incoming revenue would be immediately diverted and could not easily be withdrawn from. These accounts were: Profit, Salary, Tax and Operating Expenses.

- Three things happened almost instantly:
  - o Because there was less money available, Reilly became infinitely thriftier. He began to put a much higher value on money, time and his own worth. He began to enjoy the challenge and game of doing more with less. He became a minimalist.
  - o He became much more creative in both revenue generation and cost reduction.
  - o He discovered that profit was not a one-off event decided by an accountant at the end of a year but a daily habit.

- Neither Vinny Leahy, nor the accounting community, would be overly impressed with his modern take on GAPP. But it has transformed Reilly's financial realities and those of hundreds of business owners. It is: REVENUE - PROFITS = EXPENSES.

QUESTION

- What's your system for ending up with money in the bank each year?

29

ALWAYS CARRY CASH

Money may not be the most important thing in life but it's right on up there with oxygen.

Zig Ziglar

There are three faithful friends - an old wife, an old dog, and ready money.

Benjamin Franklin

Annual income twenty pounds, annual expenditure nineteen shillings. Result happiness.
Annual income twenty pounds, annual expenditure twenty one pounds. Result misery.

Charles Dickens, Mr. Micawber to David Copperfield

When news broke on Galway Bay FM that a Galway man called Reilly had been apprehended outside the Louvre in possession of a hoard of priceless paintings, there was consternation in the pubs of Galway.

Some were scathing of Reilly's impertinence for having been so brazen to try and rob the Louvre. I mean it was one thing robbing Kenny's, or one of the other local art galleries, but who did Reilly think he was robbing one of the most famous art museums in the world?

Most, however, were secretly in awe of his audacity, his ingenuity, and his now global profile having been caught. He was the lead news story on Sky, CNN, the BBC and, of course, Bernadette Prendergast on Galway Bay FM, who first broke the story when Reilly called her from Paris on his mobile.

As news of his artistic prowess spread, hundreds of locals resolved to go to Paris to support him in his court case.

On the day of his trial, the streets of Paris were as busy as the streets of Galway would be on a race day. There was pandemonium in the court house as the *gendarmes* tried to restrain the crowd from charging the prosecution area.

It was clear the judge felt the *frisson* and opened proceedings with what many thought was a fair and reasonable shot across the bows.

"Reilly", he boomed in French. "You are to be applauded on being *ingénieux* in evading the security systems of our most secure museum. Furthermore, your willingness to advise and consult with the French authorities on preventing further thefts to the museum has been greatly appreciated and must count in your favour for pardon.

"However, how can a man so *ingénieux* have been so careless as to run out of fuel in your getaway van?"

The crowd sensed Reilly's response would be pivotal in his efforts to secure a pardon. A hushed and subdued silence befell the courthouse and the adjoining streets.

To Reilly's credit, he grounded himself, smiled benignly at the judge, and looked the jury straight in the eye before turning to the judge.

"Your *Honeyre*", he said, in his best Inter. Cert. French accent. "I quite simply had no Monet to buy Degas to make the Van Gogh".

The crowd, heretofore boisterous and unruly, were unsure as to the subtle nuances of Reilly's response, and patently aware of the seriousness of the moment, remained as quiet as mice.

The jury, however, applauded spontaneously and approvingly.

And, as for the judge, tears rolled down his puffy pink cheeks as he declared, "*Incroyable. Formidable. Ingénieux.*

"*Monsieur Reilly, Vous êtes un ami de France; un hero d'Irlande; et vous êtes libre.*"

INSIGHTS

- In this era of technology and credit cards and plasticity, we have lost much of our psychological connection with money. Hard cash. And that can be dangerously insidious as we become less aware of our true financial reality.

- As a child, Reilly found few things as gratifying as going to the Galway races with 10 quid in his pocket, and returning home with 11, having invested liberally in lemonade, chips and the hurdy gurdies. That was real wealth.

QUESTION

- How much cash have you access to?

30

SKIN IN THE GAME

Until one is committed, there is hesitancy, the chance to draw back, always ineffectiveness. Concerning all acts of initiative (and creation), there is one elementary truth, the ignorance of which kills countless ideas and splendid plans: that the moment one definitely commits oneself, then Providence moves too.

William Hutchison Murray

Reilly and Flaherty had gone on an almighty skite after Connacht beat the Cardiff Blues in the Sportsground in February. They landed in Ward's pub four sheets to the wind and Reilly repaired to the Gents as Flaherty proceeded to put a round on at the bar.

Unfortunately, in the act of addressing the urinal, a €5 note escaped from Reilly's pocket and found its way into the flotsam and jetsam of Saturday evening's flow.

As Reilly was contemplating his response, Flaherty arrives in and assesses the situation with considerable glee.

"Now you have a bold decision to make, Reilly. What'll you do?"

Quick as a wink, Reilly whips out his wallet, extricates a €50 note, and throws it into the urinal.

Flaherty was now dumbfounded, in addition to being hammered, always a lethal combination in his case.

"You idiot. I can't believe what I've just seen. Are you just after throwing a €50 note on top of a €5 note?"

"Of course", said Reilly as if it was the most obvious thing in the world. "You didn't think I'd stick my hand in there for €5, did you?"

INSIGHTS

- The more skin you have in the game, the greater your commitment.
- In many of the crucial decisions in our lives, we arrive at a tipping point or emotional conundrum between "Will I?" or "Won't I?" Your decision is influenced greatly by your association of pain or pleasure to the outcome. Sometimes, like Reilly in this instance, we need to associate massive pain with our decision-making. When the loss was merely a fiver, there was insufficient pain to motivate him to act. When there was €55 at stake, the decision was a lot easier.
- Therefore, in order to help you be more decisive and committed, you may need to associate massive pain with not making the decision or alternatively, massive pleasure with making it.

QUESTION

- What decisions have you been procrastinating on?
- How can you motivate yourself to take action on those decisions?

31

ARE YOU ON SALARY
OR COMMISSION?

When John F. Kennedy once was asked how he became a war hero, he replied, "It was quite easy. Somebody sunk my boat".

Anon.

Reilly had driven the whole way from New Quay to Donegal Town in a blinding snowstorm. He was concerned about the weather for the next day as he had important sales appointments booked all over the county.

He was utterly knackered after the drive and repaired promptly to the bar in Harvey's Point for a quiet pint to relax himself.

"Do you think the roads will be clear enough to travel in the morning?", he enquired of Eunan, the barman.

"Well, Reilly, that all depends on whether you're on salary or commission."

INSIGHTS

- This is a great metaphor for life. As in the chicken and egg fable, it asks whether you're simply *involved in* life or truly *committed*.

- Many times, we're at our most creative and inventive when we're under pressure to perform. Pressure heightens the natural adrenaline that enables us to perform at superior levels.

- So, if the events of the pandemic (or something else) have forced you from salary to commission, it may be a blessing in disguise, if you are open and receptive to the learnings and opportunities.

- Burning your bridges or puncturing your boats also can be effective strategies.

- Get around people like Eunan. People of wisdom and wit and wherewithal who tell it to you as it is and not as how you'd like to hear it.

QUESTIONS

- In what areas in your life are you paid for by salary?
- In what areas in your life are you paid for by commission?
- What one area, if you were to commit to 100%, would make the most difference in your business or life?

32

YOU'VE BEEN MUGGED

You can't beat bought experience.

John Webb O'Rourke, serial entrepreneur

Getting mugged once was unfortunate. Getting mugged twice had to be a lesson from the Universe.

It was a miserably wet night at Dalymount Park where Bohs had just beaten Galway United 1-0 and Reilly couldn't get a taxi back into town quick enough.

It was only when he was in the taxi that he noticed his wallet with €100 in it was gone. He'd had it during the match to buy chips at half-time.

"They see the culchies coming a mile away", says the Dublin taxi-driver unsympathetically.

Reilly swore that it would never happen again and felt as safe as houses in the more salubrious surrounds of Dublin 4 after the Ireland *v* Italy rugby match a fortnight later.

And yet once again, as he was he was in deep conversation with a sound man he'd met in Doheny & Nesbitt's, he noticed that his wallet, again containing €100, was gone. Unfortunately, this time he also had a watch and an inscribed signet ring belonging to his late Father in it. Neither the watch nor the ring had any street value.

He was still fuming the next day as he was walking along St. Stephen's Green when who should sidle up beside him but the sound man he'd been having the *craic* with the evening before in Doheny & Nesbitt's.

Reilly described to him the entire saga and explained that it wasn't so much losing the money that upset him, it was the sentimental value of the watch and the ring. He'd pay anything to get them back.

When the sound man empathised with him and offered to get his watch and ring back for as little as €500, it was then that Reilly heard the first tinkle announcing a lesson from the Universe.

He was in the presence of a professional.

They haggled and haggled and eventually the sound man came down from his high horse and acquiesced to accepting the €80 cash remaining in Reilly's pocket. In return, Reilly received a ticket to a pawn shop where he could retrieve his watch and ring.

Although Reilly would later have to pay a further €70 to get back the watch and ring, he was secretly proud of the hard bargain he'd driven with the thief.

Reilly was still figuring out what the message from the Universe was when the mugger took out one of Reilly's business cards that had also been in the wallet.

"I see you give business courses to entrepreneurs and have a new SMACHT programme starting at the end of March", says the mugger. "I've checked you out online and I'm prepared to deliver the session on Finance & Profitability for you at a very attractive fee. Your clients can be guaranteed they'll learn income-generating strategies that no business professor will ever teach and that will generate serious returns for their business."

Reilly didn't doubt it and signed him up on the spot.

INSIGHTS

- Compare and contrast the outcomes of the two muggers.
- Mugger number one made a straight €100 cash and will never see his victim again.
- Mugger number two, applying effective income-generating strategies, made €100 on the mugging; €70 in the pawn shop; and €80 selling the pawn ticket back to Reilly. Total income: €250. In addition he acquired a satisfied customer, who will continue to do business with him for many years and will most likely refer him to dozens more successful entrepreneurs who would like to generate more money.
- Almost every industry is characterised by industry-standard approaches to generating income. For example, most retailers advertise in local papers; manufacturers use direct sales teams; doctors, dentists and solicitors rely on referrals; stockbrokers do practically all their business on the phone; and most thieves just mug you, take the money and run for it.
- But the professionals. They have a unique approach all of their own that maximises profitability and customer satisfaction. They understand implicitly the meaning of value and charge accordingly.
- Always be asking for business. The pros do.

QUESTION

- What other ways could you generate more income?

33

FLY FIRST CLASS

If you travel first class, you think first class and you are more likely to play first class.

Raymond Floyd

Although it's nigh on 40 years ago, Reilly will always remember the day he flew First Class for the first time. He'd just joined the Priority Management organisation as a young and innocent time management trainer and was *en route* from Vancouver to Quebec for their annual training conference.

As luck would have it, he was seated beside Dan Stamp, the President of the organisation.

Dan, then and now, lives life as if he's just emerged from the pages of Dale Carnegie's classic *How to Win Friends and Influence People.*

Everyone loves Dan: associates; board members; clients; members of the press; suppliers; workshop attendees; men; women; and children. He simply exudes emotional intelligence.

The first thing Dan does on taking his seat on the aircraft is to press the flight assistance button, summoning assistance. Bing-bong.

A taciturn air hostess – called Darlene according to her name-tag – was clearly unimpressed with Dan's enthusiasm, and promptly informs him: "Cabin assistance does not commence until after take-off".

Unperturbed, Dan informs Darlene that all himself and Reilly want are two comment cards on which to provide feedback on the quality of the flight.

With the sweetest of smiles – you know the one that is a cross between sympathy and 'Stop your messing now' – Darlene tells the lads: "Passenger comment cards are only distributed at the end of the flight, when passengers have an experience to comment on".

With an equally syrupy smile, Dan assures her that he understands her reasoning but nonetheless, he'd welcome two comment cards, now.

To say his request caused a modicum of consternation amongst the cabin-crew was an understatement.

As she reluctantly retreated to get the forms, Darlene was joined by a gaggle of other flight attendants who were now giving Reilly and Dan the proverbial 'daggers'.

Upon getting the forms, Dan counselled Reilly to copy closely the sentiment of his comments. Having ticked every superlative rating for Quality, Service, Safety and Comfort, Dan proceeded to write in qualitative detail about the excellence of the flight experience.

"I travel the world regularly on business and the level of customer service provided on airlines is a source of great passion for me.

Frequently, I'm disappointed. But I must say the quality of service on this flight stands out as one of the best I've ever experienced."

He went on to cite a number of specific examples about the food, the ambience, and the comfort.

Finally, he wrote that "the cheerfulness, care and charm of Darlene (the air hostess) was second to none" and that she espoused perfectly the passenger care ethos of the airline as documented on their mission statement.

Just as the pilot switched on the 'fasten your seat belts sign' and instructed the cabin crew to prepare for take-off, Dan once again pressed the 'bing-bong' switch and cheerfully presented the seething Darlene with the two completed comment cards.

Fifteen minutes after take-off, Dan and Reilly were upgraded to First Class.

INSIGHTS

- The message from this post is not to provide insincere feedback in order to blag upgrades, although that can very much be a bonus. It is to make us aware of the power of positive expectation. Let people know in advance that you expect the best from them and watch their performance soar.

- Next time you visit your accountant, dentist, doctor or any other service provider, inform them at the outset how highly you regard them and how you expect them to be of wonderful service to you.

- This week, resolve to fly first class everywhere you go.

QUESTIONS

James Clear, author of *Atomic Habits*, claims to write 'the most wisdom per word of any newsletter on the web'.

Reilly has to agree.

James' post this Thursday on the power of questions is apposite: 'The questions you ask yourself will largely determine the answers you get'.

Ask yourself:

- ○ 'Why am I not successful?' You'll get answers that berate you.

- ○ 'How can I succeed here?' You'll get answers that push you.

The bottom line is to be deliberate in the questions you ask yourself.

POSTSCRIPT

Fergus Foley, founder and proprietor of The Blue Cloak chain of fashion shops, was probably the best fashion retailer Reilly ever knew.

Gerry Meehan, former President of the Irish Dental Association, was probably the best dentist Reilly ever knew.

Both are now passed on to greener pastures where Reilly has no doubt they continue to share stories and wisdom.

Fergus once confided to Reilly the secret to getting superior service or 'flying first class'.

"Reilly, when I go in to Gerry Meehan's surgery, the first thing I say is 'Gerry, I know you're the best dentist in Galway. I expect you to do a wonderful job on my teeth today'."

Gerry Meehan also once confided to Reilly.

"Reilly, every time Fergus Foley comes in to my surgery, without fail, he tells me that I'm the best dentist in Galway and he expects me to do a wonderful job on his teeth. And although I'd like to think I do my best for every one of my patients, I have to admit I give him that bit extra."

Leaba i measc na naingeal agus na naomh ag an mbeirt.

34

ONE OF A KIND

Figure out who you are; then do it on purpose.

Dolly Parton

*The quickest way to sell anything to
anyone is to tell them they can't have it.*

Arthur Daly

*The day I put an end to unlimited availability
was the day I took back control of my life.*

A great client of Reilly's (who understandably wishes to be anonymous)

R eilly's Uncle Stiofáin was an avid stamp collector. When the fishing season drew to a close in late October, he'd pack away his rods and his boat and effortlessly transfer his full and undivided attention to the care and maintenance of his beloved stamp collection.

Over hours on end, he'd explain to Reilly the quality and value and significance of each of the stamps in his collection. In addition, he'd counsel him on building the collection's value.

"It's like all the great football teams, Reilly. Each year, the great managers identify a few new 'All Stars' and they let go a few former greats. It's the same with stamps. You should always be looking out for some new tasty specimens and moving on some of your former darlings."

In order to identify 'tasty specimens', Uncle Stiofáin subscribed to a number of stamp collector magazines. Many's the winter evening Reilly whiled away the hours with him looking through them.

On one particular evening, Stiofáin became visibly excited upon reading of 'The Last Will and Testament of One Randolph Tucker Gladstone, late of Missouri, USA'.

It appeared that the late Randy had been the proud owner of a '1902 Ben Franklin one cent green stamp in mint condition valued at $170'. Back in 1970, $170 was serious dough.

"*Trócaire Dé ar a anam dílis* (God's mercy on his soul) but Randy and I have been long awaiting this day when one or the other of us would bite the dust first.

"It's a fair price, Reilly, but never offer what they initially ask. We'll telegram a bid of $149 in the morning and let the good Lord himself look after the details."

A few weeks later, Stiofáin informed Reilly that his offer had been accepted and that the stamp had arrived. He'd wait until Reilly was present to open it. Reilly couldn't wait to get out from school to go and view it.

Stiofáin met him in the front room of 14 St. Mary's Road, where he had the green table they used for playing cards laid out theatrically in the middle of the room.

Stiofáin had a pair of gloves for everything. A pair of nylon gloves for tying flies. A wire pair for pulling baits out of the jaws of big pike. A pair of tan calf-leather ones used for driving. But, for handling his stamps, he only ever used white silk gloves.

Donning these, he opened the envelope containing the stamp. The drama was lost on Reilly.

He was never as deflated as when Stiofáin placed that *stampeen* on a large sheet of white paper in the middle of the card table.

Tears appeared in both their eyes – but for different reasons.

Reilly was genuinely devastated and gutted for Stiofáin. Imagine that he'd shelled out $149 for this piece of paper that was scarcely a half-inch square and insipid in every feature down to Ben Franklin's lifeless face.

From his own stamp collection, Stiofáin gently withdrew a stamp of his own and placed it reverently beside Randy's. To Reilly's amazement and astonishment, it was exactly the same in every feature.

For such a giant of a man, Stiofáin became strangely ethereal and otherworldly.

"Reilly, you are now in the presence of the two last remaining one cent Ben Franklin stamps in the world. *An rud is annamh is iontach* (What's rare is wonderful).

"Now, I want you to do me a favour."

Taking a packet of Maguire & Patterson matches from his pocket, he said: "Reilly, I want you to take Randy's stamp there and burn it".

"You're having a laugh, Uncle Stiofáin. Why on earth would anybody want to burn something as rare and valuable as this stamp?"

"Do it and you'll understand."

And Reilly did. Slowly and carefully and deliberately.

He lit the match the way he'd been taught to light a match on a squally day up the lake. Cupping it in the palm of his hand, he tilted the head down so that it burned evenly and brightly. He then placed the flame beneath a corner of the stamp so that it too would burn evenly and brightly.

For one fleeting second, it appeared as if even Ben Franklin's colourless face lit up. As the stamp curled into a foil of grey ash, Reilly understood for the first time the meaning of the ancient Irish phrase his Uncle Stiofáin had just quoted.

Stiofáin, being the consummate teacher that he was, didn't have to tell Reilly that scarcity creates value. One unique stamp is worth infinitely more than two rare stamps combined.

INSIGHTS

There are three key learnings here:

- Scarcity, or limitation, creates value. Build scarcity deep into the foundations of your time commitments.
- Stop trying to be like everybody else and instead become the only stamp of 'You' in the world. You can be the only 'You' in the planet's population of seven billion. The more 'You' you become, the more attractive you become to just about everyone and everything.
- Murder your darlings. Review all your commitments and resolve to sever those that are unproductive, unprofitable and unfulfilling.

QUESTIONS

- Have you figured out who you are?
- If so, are you doing it on purpose?
- What current commitments, that are causing you stress, will you jettison forever this week?

35

THE ULTIMATE
WEALTH CREATION
DISCIPLINE

Be like a postage stamp.
Stick to one thing until you get there.

Josh Billings

One of the things about being in the mentoring game is that people are always asking you for your opinion on their ideas. After once telling Ray O'Connor that he didn't think the Connemarathon (now one of the most prestigious marathon events in the world) would ever be a runner Reilly made it a unequivocal rule of his never ever to dispense an opinion on a business idea ever again.

So when Flaherty sidled up to him in the pub last night and said: "Reilly, I have a cracker of an idea. Keep it to yourself but I'm thinking of setting up a portable sauna business. It's a thing of beauty. What d'ya think?", Reilly politely replied: "I think ideas are greatly overrated".

"Oh, come on, Reilly. You're so negative, I could kill you. What d'ya really think?"

Reilly was tired and cranky after a long day and in no humour to pander to Flaherty and yet another one of his great ideas. He gave it to him straight.

"That's precisely your problem, Flaherty. Thinking, not doing. You spend too much time thinking. And simply thinking up great ideas doesn't make them happen.

"Thinking about killing me doesn't make you a murderer. Nor does thinking about Jennifer Aniston – as you tell me you do all the time – make you her boyfriend. And neither does thinking about business ideas make you a business person.

"Think CREATION NOT IDEATION.

"Creation derives from the Latin word *creare* which means 'to create' or 'to bring into being'.

"You were sent into this world to create, Flaherty, not just to think.

"But creating – bringing an idea to the marketplace and adding value – requires focus, tenacity and *smacht*, Flaherty – qualities you've never demonstrated in any abundance.

"The anatomy of any successful business proceeds through a journey from idea to research to beta model to commercial model to remarkable product. You rarely venture beyond the idea phase."

Flaherty might have listened but for the arrival into the pub of 12 stunners clearly away on a hen night. Excusing himself from Reilly, he said. "Thanks for listening, Reilly. You're spot on. There's a time to ideate and a time to create. And right now I've got creation firmly on my mind".

The first thing that Reilly noticed the following morning on his walk for his swim was the whiff of woodsmoke, with maybe tones of lavender and sandalwood.

The next was a crudely-made wooden sign, proclaiming:

SAUNA FOR THE SOUL
€20 per session.

And right out on the Quay was an even more crudely-made wooden edifice athwart Flaherty's farm trailer, being fuelled by a log fire.

And, *quelle surprise*, but who was on the Quay but Flaherty and he surrounded by the 12 girls from the hen party disrobing from their dry robes and entering Flaherty's SAUNA FOR THE SOUL.

Reilly was impressed and admitted as much to Flaherty: "Not bad, Flaherty, as business models go. You'll earn €240 for an hour's input with indirect expenses totaling not much more than €50 and, with a provision of 10% for fixed costs, you should wash a good €150 for your day's work".

"Ah, that's the thin end of the wedge, Reilly. After the sauna, I bring them on a guided walk of the Flaggy Shore. That's €250 clear. And then I transport them to Doolin for entertainment. That's very profitable, as I get a cut of the action from the various establishments I bring them to and these girls like to party. And, finally, tonight I'm organising a private dinner for them in Dunguaire Castle. As that's a once-in-a-lifetime experience for any bride-to-be, I can name my price for that."

Reilly was clearly astounded at Flaherty's 'Creation' but was still slow to praise him.

"One swallow never made a summer, Flaherty. You might have struck it lucky today but it's a long season."

"Ah, that's the thing, Reilly. Seven of the party are getting married this year and five have already privately booked me as their Henner. And when I fulfil their Henning needs with aplomb, I'll connect with dozens of other Henning opportunities.

"I call it 'The Ultimate Wealth Creation Strategy'.

"It's a thing of beauty, Reilly."

INSIGHTS

- Business is very simple. All you ever need are some hungry customers and a solution to their needs.

- The only two things people ever buy are solutions to problems and good feelings. Make sure you do both.

- Find someone to challenge you to take action and create something.

- Find a niche and penetrate it. Become the 'Henner of choice' for your niche.

- Don't wait until everything is right to launch your idea. Just get out there; promote yourself; and improve your offering a little every day.

- A day will eventually arrive when you too will have a 'thing of beauty'.

QUESTIONS

- Do you know of any 'hungry' customers?

- How could you solve their problem or make them feel good?

- What niche could you penetrate?

HUMAN
BEINGS

36

YOU WON'T BE WITH US LONG

You know it's time to sell when the shoeshine boy gives you stock tips.

Joe Kennedy on being advised by his shoeshine boy to "Buy Hindenburg".

Every day, and in every way, I am getting better and better.

Émile Coué

Reilly's cousin, Jack Coen, had a deep aversion to anything in a white coat. On those rare occasions when presenting before one, he insisted on Reilly accompanying him. Even then, it would not be without incident.

Some years ago, Jack's GP referred him to a dermatologist in Galway to get a second opinion on a mole on his hand. Jack was a notorious hypochondriac and instantly feared the worst.

As luck would have it, the dermatologist was Hannah Moriarty who'd grown up in town with Reilly. Hannah was the nearest thing to a genius Reilly had met, but she was painfully shy and withdrawn. Reilly had once accompanied her to a Med Ball when no one else would. Even then, she had to be home at 11pm to be up for an anatomy lecture in the morning. That was the type she was.

She brightened up visibly when she saw Reilly in the waiting room. This was long before the outbreak of excessive GDPR, so Reilly tactfully took her aside and explained the position regarding Jack.

"Look, Hannah, he's as tough as nails on the outside but, inside, he's a pussy cat. If the mole is sinister, will you gild the lily a *biteen*? You can tell me the real truth after and I'll convert it to Jack-ese for him."

Reilly had scarcely settled himself to read the *Connacht Tribune* when Jack bolted out of the consulting room, followed closely by a coterie of mystified medics, including Hannah.

Jack then declared to the entire waiting room: "If I am going to die, it'll be in The Sliding Rock and not the Regional Hospital".

"What's the story, Hannah?", said Reilly, clearly rattled. "What did you tell him?"

"Reilly, I examined the mole thoroughly under a microscope and I am confident it is a junctional melanocytic nevi."

Reilly felt himself buckle at the knees.

"I explained to Mr. Coen that it was absolutely benign, and that because I knew you, I'd remove it there and then and that he wouldn't be with us long."

Reilly looked kindly into Hannah's innocent eyes of blue. He'd often been tempted to suggest to her that she might have specialised in pathology or some other branch of medicine that didn't require as much interaction with live people. But then, that was none of his business.

By the time, he'd tracked Jack down in The Sliding Rock, Jack had already downed a half wan and a full pint of porter.

"I'm goosed, Reilly. I'm benign and I won't be with you long. Those were exactly the words that young doctor told me."

And beckoning Ulick the barman over, Jack proclaimed: "I've confided the prognosis to Ulick. Ulick here has seen it all. Ulick is dealing with more people from the hospital every day than the doctors themselves. D'ya know what he says, Reilly? It's the benign ones that never come back to The Sliding Rock. It's only ever the malignant ones that keep coming back. Isn't that right, Ulick?"

It took Reilly another six pints and six half wans to convince Jack that 'benign' was good and that his mole was harmless.

Then there was the time Jack was referred for a stress test to a cardiologist. This time, he insisted that Reilly come into the consulting rooms with him. The deal was that the cardiologist would not communicate one word with Jack whatsoever, but would break the news privately to Reilly whilst Jack was in residence with Ulick in The Sliding Rock.

Following a 15-minute stint on a treadmill where he was connected to a battery of monitors, Jack vanished and the cardiologist peered down his nose condescendingly at Reilly.

"I recognise you. You're the mullicker who played for UCG the day you pipped us in that God-awful pitch called the Sportsground. Do you remember me? I was the Trinity winger that day", said the cardiologist haughtily.

"Oh, I remember you well", said Reilly warmly. "In fact, everyone in UCG still remembers you. We christened you 'Hot Dinner'."

"Oh, I wasn't that special, was I? Why ever did you call me 'Hot Dinner'?"

"'Cause you couldn't tackle one."

That all but concluded the pleasantries and the cardiologist cut to the chase on Jack's prognosis.

"Your cousin is grossly overweight; smokes too much; drinks too much; worries too much; has high blood pressure; high cholesterol; and has an abysmal family history of chronic heart disease.

"Mr. Reilly, I doubt very much your cousin and I will be seeing each other again, at least in this world. My receptionist will settle the bill with you on your way out."

What Reilly did next was morally wrong. In fact, it was downright illegal. But it was fully premeditated. His Auntie Mary had always taught him to do the right thing because it was right. So he did.

Jack had once again consumed a half wan and a pint of porter and had the same again colouring the counter before Reilly appeared.

"Break it to me straight, Reilly. Sudden death doesn't scare me", says Jack, anything but convincingly.

"Jack, that ponce of a cardiologist can't believe it but your stress test was textbook. Although you're overweight and drink too much, you've the heart of a man 20 years younger. He never wants to see you again."

Jack digested the prognosis deferentially. Suddenly, and without warning, he stood up, pushed the unfinished pint back and proclaimed to Reilly.

"Come on, Reilly. We're going out on the Prom for a good brisk walk. Pubs are no place for healthy people."

And that was the epiphany that precipitated Jack's conversion to vibrant health. He continued walking on a daily basis; gave up the fags and booze; and lived another 20 years without ever once returning to that cardiologist.

INSIGHTS

- Words are veritable wizards' wands. They can cure as decisively as they can kill. Choose yours carefully and judiciously in all matters of business, career and relationships.

- Bring a good listener with you to meetings of particular importance, be they business, financial or medical. Sometimes, during moments of intense emotional stress, we can mishear and misinterpret the meaning of the spoken words.

- Great communicators tend to avoid industry-specific jargon and communicate in words and images that their listener understands.

- Eschew confiding with the 'Ulicks' of this world for information regarding important decisions. Seek out experts in their field, and if necessary, be prepared to pay for good information.

- Do the right thing because it's right.
- Your beliefs are literally things. Those who believe they are abundant in beauty, money and vibrant health generally are. Émile Coué, a French pharmacist, popularised the notion of the Placebo Principle at the beginning of the 20th century. He would, Reilly-like, dupe his patients into thinking that they were taking a powerful drug that would cure their ailment. And in many cases, it did – even though it only contained chalk dust. The placebo is considered unethical by the GDPR brigade. It is still used extensively, however, by leading drugs manufacturers in clinical trials.

QUESTIONS

- What words of magic could you use to uplift someone today? Hint: most are simple, like "Well done", "You look great", "Thank you", "I believe in you" or "You can and you will".
- What words of destruction might you be using on a continual basis that may be bringing people down?
- Who are examples of people who impress you by how they can use simple language to convey powerful messages?
- Who are the 'Ulicks' in your life?

37

THE POWER OF BELIEF

You'll never soar with the eagles if you continue to scratch with the chickens.

Zig Ziglar

It had taken Reilly all of three years to train his Labrador, Potter, not to retrieve the fowl oven-ready. And today, for the first time, the *smacht* had paid off.

In a clump of heather, beneath a sheer cliff face in the Burren, Potter displayed textbook behaviour.

His tail arched and pointed to the sky, alerting Reilly to the exact location of their prey. With his eyes, he mesmerised the bird into a state of total immobilisation, like a rabbit blinded in the glare of a headlight. All he needed was the command from Reilly, and the bird was as good as in the bag.

Potter could be forgiven for not knowing it was midsummer, and that Reilly's gun was safely ensconced at home in its security case awaiting the opening of the shooting season in September. He was singularly unimpressed when Reilly gently ushered him aside and stooped to see what he'd discovered.

There, amidst the fronds of heather, was a magnificent bird of prey. It peered out at them with beautiful, but terrified, eyes of amber yellow. One of its wings hung limply by its side. Clearly, it had fallen from the cliffs overhead and had been abandoned by its mother.

Instinctively, Reilly thought of Ronan Byrne, the Friendly Farmer. No one in Ireland knows more about birds and their well-being. He resolved to get the bird to Ronan *tout suite*.

"It's an eagle chick and it's in bad shape. The best that we can do with it now is put it in with the other chickens and let nature take its course", said Ronan empathetically.

And that's precisely what happened. They christened the eagle chick Iolar, the Irish word for an eagle, and over the proceeding weeks and months she flourished. She got on like the proverbial house on fire with the other hens and chickens.

In time, she learned to peck like a chicken, scratch like a chicken, strut like a chicken. She even succeeded in clucking and cackling like a chicken when one of the others laid an egg.

And then one day, a large shadow appeared over the chicken farm in Athenry. Iolar and the other chickens paused momentarily from scratching and looked up to see a majestic bird glide over the farm.

"What's that?", said Iolar, in awe.

"That's an eagle", said one of the elder and wiser chickens.

"Wow. I'd give anything to fly and soar like that", said Iolar.

"You can't", said another older and even wiser chicken. "You're a chicken, and chickens can't fly. That there is the king of all birds. Now put your head down, lest the eagle see you and take you away".

Iolar dutifully began to scratch the ground again but couldn't take her mind off the spectacular specimen she had just seen.

Some days after, the big eagle happened to be cruising the vicinity of the farm again, and with the aid of his 'eagle eye', he was stunned to see what he perceived to be the cutest eagle he'd ever seen – hanging out with a bunch of chickens. He surged earthwards with such velocity that the chickens scarcely had time to make the safety of the chicken coop.

Alas, not Iolar. She was so enthralled by the power and splendour of the eagle that she stood transfixed and rooted to the ground.

"What are you doing here?", asked the big eagle, curiously but gently.

"What are you getting at?", replied Iolar with false bravado.

"What are you doing hanging out with a bunch of chickens?"

"I am a chicken. They are my friends. They are my family. They took me in when my mother abandoned me. They've taught me everything I know", said Iolar defiantly.

"You're not a chicken. You're an eagle. You're the king of all birds. From Caesar to Hitler, you are revered as the ultimate symbol of power. You belong in the sky, not in the dirt."

"Nonsense", shrieked Iolar. "I'm no eagle. I can't even fly."

"You can't fly because you've never tried, and you've never been coached by someone who can. Come with me to the cliff at the edge of the farm and I'll teach you to fly like an eagle."

From the recesses of the chicken coop, Iolar heard a rising cacophony of chicken-speak from the other chickens.

"Don't listen to him", chorused the frantic chickens. "He's a liar, a spoofer and a womaniser. If you go with him, you'll never come back. If you jump from that cliff, you'll surely die. Stay with us here where everything is cosy and safe."

Iolar looked back at her adopted family and friends and tears welled up in her eyes of amber gold. She thought of all the great times she had scratching in the dirt and scurrying away from Ronan when he tried to tuck them in at night safe from the fox.

But deep within her being was a knowing calling. A calling to be more. To do more. To have more. To fly – who knows, even to soar.

She bravely gave the other chickens the wings up and followed the other eagle out of the farmyard and up to the cliff.

At the cliff summit, the other eagle caringly put its wing around Iolar's graceful shoulders and pointed out all the wonders of an eagle's world. To the north was Croagh Patrick and the Twelve Pins and to the south were the majestic peaks of the Magillicuddy Reeks. Iolar felt an intense stirring in her loins.

Then the other eagle jumped – and effortlessly glided on a series of invisible thermals that powerfully supported his body. Iolar marvelled at such unadulterated freedom. She dearly wished to do likewise.

She looked down, however, and all she saw were the sharp and treacherous rocks hundreds of feet below. She heard once again, the clarion cry of the other chickens squawking, "If you jump from that cliff, you'll surely die".

"Look to the sun. Throw your heart over the cliff and let me guide you every flap of the way", said the other eagle encouragingly.

And she did.

And as she soared, her triumphant cry reverberated joyously around the walls of the chicken coop in Athenry.

INSIGHTS

- Beliefs are to your mind what software is to your computer: the programmes that condition and predicate your entire destiny. And your beliefs are fashioned and fossilised in the 'chicken yards' of your life.

- If you ever believed that you're not old enough, smart enough, or good looking enough – then it's quite likely you've been got at by 'chicken yard beliefs'.

- Genetically, we are born to win but quickly become programmed to lose.

QUESTION

- Are you soaring with the eagles or scratching with the chickens? (As Zig Ziglar reminded us, 'you'll never soar with the eagles if you continue to scratch with the chickens'. It's your choice.)

38

BEWARE SURPRISES

Beat the news home ...•

The best surprise is no surprise.

Holiday Inns' slogan

• When Reilly was young, and they'd inadvertently break a window, the smart
thinking always was to… 'beat the news home'. Reilly never forgot it.

On his way home from a hard day's work on Friday, Reilly stopped off at Annie Nolan's Veg Box in Finavarra to pick up the weekly veggies.

He ended up getting more than he bargained for. Annie's the ultimate salesperson and proceeded to assemble a bouquet of fresh flowers before his very eyes.

"There are some red roses for the heart. Some tiger lilies for the mind. Some lily-of-the-valley for the body. And, of course, some wild lavender for the passion. You'll surely surprise Mrs. Reilly with this bunch!"

He didn't give it a second thought.

"Surprise", he beckoned to Mrs. Reilly, as he positioned the bouquet on the table centrepiece.

And it certainly was. She went for him head-on.

"I've had the day from Hell. First, I ran out of petrol on the way to school and was half an hour late getting there. When I got there, the kids were like bags of cats all day long. And then, when I came home I dropped my mother's porcelain bowl and it's in smithereens on the kitchen floor.

"And now, on top of all that, you come home drunk."

INSIGHTS

- Beware surprises in business and life.
- Although often well-intentioned, as a general rule, your customers don't like them. Your staff don't like them. Even your nearest and dearest don't always like them.
- Beware of acting on impulse. For sure, on any given day, you can emerge smelling of roses, but all too often, your impulsive actions can backfire and end up getting you in trouble.
- It sounds boring and oh so conservatively prudent, but a policy of 'no surprises' towards all and sundry makes for sound business and life sense.

QUESTIONS

- What areas in your business and life are causing surprises?

39

BEWARE
ASSUMPTIONS

Beware assuming. It can make an ass out of you and me.

Anon.

It surprised nobody that Ned Duggan ended up as a Bishop. All throughout their school days, he was cerebral, serious, disciplined and of course, celibate.

Conversely, it surprised few that Reilly failed to pursue an ecclesiastical calling. In matters of personality profile, the Bishop was more 'saint' to Reilly's 'rogue.'

They did, however, share a mutual love for fishing and shooting. And on 1 November every year, the opening of the pheasant season, the two would embark on an annual pilgrimage to the bogs and woods of Ballyglunin.

They'd meet at the Bishop's Palace at daybreak and after a hearty breakfast of porridge, bacon and scones, they'd be well foddered for the task at hand.

For a solid five hours, along with Reilly's Labrador Potter, they'd scour hazel woods, fields of uncut beet, *móinteach* bog with heather as high as your eyes, and, of course, Knockdoe Hill. Rarely if ever did Knockdoe fail to rise a bird or two if you knew where to look, and Reilly and the Bishop knew where the birds lay.

Following the hunt, they'd repair to the Palace for lunch and that was a lunch worth working for.

There'd be a smoked salmon starter, followed by a *consommé* soup; roast fillet beef; crème caramel, and a cheese board.

Maybe it was the Chateauneuf-du-Pape, but last year during the meal Reilly couldn't help noticing a certain *frisson* between the Bishop and his new housekeeper. The Bishop was always an intuitive type and sensed Reilly's drift.

"Reilly, I can guess what you're thinking, but I assure you our relationship is purely platonic."

A few days later, the housekeeper noticed that the antique solid silver soup ladle that had served three Popes had gone missing. She instantly put two and two together and insisted to the Bishop that Reilly must be the culprit.

"I doubt it very much", said the Bishop. "I've known Reilly for 40 years and whilst he's a rogue and a scoundrel, he's no thief. However, to assuage your mind, I'll put it to him."

So the Bishop penned a hombre-to-hombre letter to Reilly:

> *Dear Reilly,*
> *I am not saying that 'you did' take the solid silver soup ladle from*
> *my Palace, and I am not saying that 'you did not' take the solid*
> *silver spoon ladle from my Palace, but the fact of the matter is that*
> *the ladle has been missing since your visit.*

Reilly always believed in negotiating a contentious situation head-on and so he duly replied:

> *Your Grace,*
> *I am not saying that 'you do' sleep with your housekeeper, and I*
> *am not saying that 'you do not' sleep with your housekeeper, but*
> *the fact of the matter is that if you were sleeping in your own bed,*
> *you would have found the ladle by now.*

INSIGHTS

- Beware making assumptions. As you've no doubt heard on every training course you've ever attended, 'an assumption can make an ass out of you and me'.
- Comeuppance is an old-fashioned and quirky word for 'a punishment or fate that someone deserves'. The Bishop got his comeuppance in the end for his arrogance and deceit, as most people ultimately do.
- Creative thinking is still the mother of skills.

QUESTIONS

- What assumptions are you basing your business on?

40

WHO'S MARKING YOU?

Don't wish it was easier, wish you were better.
Don't wish for fewer problems, wish for more skills.
Don't wish for less challenge, wish for more wisdom.

Jim Rohn

Don't join an easy crowd; you won't grow. Go where the
expectations and the demands to perform are high.

Jim Rohn

Crush Adidas.

**Nike's original two-word mission statement when it was still
just an upstart, operating out of a garage.**

Reilly hadn't missed either a league or championship hurling match that Galway had played since God was a lad. And in his unequivocal opinion, John Connolly was the finest hurler of his era.

So it came to pass that, when Connolly eventually retired after 15 arduous years playing at inter-county level where he won both club and county All-Irelands, nothing would do Reilly than to introduce him to the royal and ancient small-ball game of golf.

Reilly was a handy golfer and rather fancied himself to school the hurler in the more subtle nuances of the game.

He arranged for John to join him at Oranmore Golf Links and completed a foursome with two other tasty single-figure-handicapped golfers.

As the lads were strutting their stuff and making elaborate shapes and swings on the first tee, John was busily signing autographs for a bunch of young kids. Playing golf seemed to be the last thing on his mind.

As John had never played before, the lads were lavish in their advice and profuse in their encouragement.

"Keep your head down, Johneen, and let the ball do the work for you", said Tom Nolan, a former professional golfer and good hurler in his day too.

"Forget about the howling wind; keep your left arm straight; and avoid bending your wrists too much", counselled Mike Ford, a deadly snooker player and experienced golfer.

The two lads, cute out, and aware of the vicious south-westerly wind driving in from the Atlantic each played it low and safe and both found lies close to the fairway a good 200 yards from the tee.

Reilly had been planning this day for some time and choose it to launch his spanking new Big Bertha which he'd procured on a recent trip to St. Andrews. It didn't let him down. He edged a good 40 yards beyond the lads.

Now, as John's turn beckoned, Reilly was torn between apprehension and excitement. He wanted with all his heart for John to do well but he also wanted to win. His good nature eventually got the better of him and he magnanimously offered John the use of his new Big Bertha.

"Reilly, doesn't everyone know that shiny shoes won't help you walk any faster. I'll use this old three iron one of the kids gave me."

Much to the amusement of the three 'Galacticos', John declined to use a tee. He simply tossed the ball on the ground and, without as much as a practice shot, he drove that ball 300 yards down the fairway, straight as a die.

Reilly was quickest to compose himself.

"How did you do that, Connolly? We've never seen the like before."

"Why wouldn't I?", said John. "Sure there was nobody marking me!"

INSIGHTS

- For all his illustrious hurling career, John Connolly had been double-marked, occasionally triple-marked, but always was a marked man. He was well-accustomed to digs in the ribs, slaps on the hands and abuse in his ears.

- Being the consummate professional that he was, John accepted hard marking as part and parcel of the game and learned to accept it, adapt to it and thrive on it.

- In many ways, hard marking is what refines us and, ultimately, defines us. Stiff competition is the very mother of mastery and excellence.

- Every successful industry is characterised by the existence of at least two dominant competitors: think Pepsi and Coke; Nike and Adidas; Supermac's and McDonald's. Although bitter rivals, their competition brings out the best in each other's respective performance and grows the demand for their produce.

QUESTION

- Who (what competitors) will you choose to have mark you?

41

GONE TO CONGO

I've met a lot of leaders in the Army who were very competent — but they didn't have character. And for every job they did well, they sought reward in the form of promotions, in the form of awards and decorations, in the form of getting ahead at the expense of someone else, in the form of another piece of paper that awarded them another degree — a sure road to the top. You see, these were competent people, but they lacked character. I've also met a lot of leaders who had superb character but who lacked competence. They weren't willing to pay the price of leadership, to go the extra mile because that's what it took to be a great leader. And that's sort of what it's all about. To lead in the 21st century, to take soldiers, sailors, airmen into battle, you will be required to have both character and competence.

US Army General H. Norman Schwarzkopf

P at Carroll was the Commander of the first platoon of Irish troops to go to the Congo in 1961. More crucially, he brought them all home safely, without as much as a flea-bite, six months later. He was also about the wisest man Reilly had ever met.

One evening over libations in Garavan's, he explained to Reilly what it took to lead men into war and return them home safely.

"The first activity of a leader is to define the roles necessary for a successful outcome. Reilly, what do you think the most important role in an army going to war is?"

Reilly was strictly more into officers' daughters than military strategy and found himself struggling for an answer.

"I suppose you'd want a few good lieutenants to lead the guys and plenty of good scrappers to do the rough stuff", said Reilly hopefully.

"Reilly, the first person every effective army leader recruits is a cook. Never forget that an army marches on its stomach.

"The second activity of a leader is to recruit someone for that role who has both competence and character. You see, Reilly, there are lots of cooks who are competent. They can cook to *cordon bleu* standards in the comfort of a custom-built kitchen but they may lack the character to do that in the jungle with bullets whizzing all around them. And I've known lots of great characters who couldn't boil an egg.

"When word arrived from de Valera to assemble a platoon forthwith to go to the Congo the first man I called was Ned Sullivan. Sullivan was the best cook in the Western Command and the first person you'd want in the trenches beside you.

"'Sullivan', I said. 'Can you prepare to depart for the Congo within the next two hours?'

"'Yes, sir', said Sullivan without flinching, and he departed promptly to his house in Renmore Road to collect his belongings.

"It was a beautiful summer's day and Sullivan's wife had taken the kids to Ballyloughane beach to avail of the clement weather. She'd tacked a note to the door saying in big letters 'Gone to Ballyloughane'.

"Sullivan collected his kit and caboodle, untacked the note from the front door, and wrote on the reverse side: 'Gone to Congo'.

"Some days later, Pat's wife met Sullivan's wife outside the Garrison Church after Mass and asked her about Sullivan.

"'Oh, he'd never discuss Army affairs with me. That's private and confidential. What I do know is that he's gone to some place called Congo.

But distance won't bother Sullivan. He's a real soldier. He once spent two whole weeks in Finner Camp up in County Donegal.'"

INSIGHTS

- In building a successful team of any nature, first define the roles necessary to achieve a successful outcome. The late Stephen Covey recommended a wonderful assignment to complete at the start of each week: outline your roles for the coming week – for example, producer, salesperson, accountant, marketeer, HR. Then assign some goals to each role. It takes only minutes but provides direction, focus and accountability for the week.

- Second, in selecting a candidate for any position, select for both competence and character. Many will have one or the other. Few will have both.

- Professionals – those with character and competence – get on with the job with a minimum of drama. Sullivan would never use four words where three would suffice.

- For what it's worth, ex-army people and nurses make great businesspeople simply because they understand systems. And that's what characterises the great ones.

QUESTIONS

- What roles do you need in your business to survive and thrive?
- Are you a person of character and competence?
- What areas of character and competence do you need to grow in?
- How much drama surrounds your business and life?

42

WHY IT'S NEVER TOO LATE TO WIN AN ALL IRELAND

It's never too late to be who you might have been.

George Eliot

By the time Sean Murphy left Roscrea College, he had two All Ireland medals to his name. In 1959 and 1960, he was the Leinster and All Ireland Senior Schools Pole Vaulting Champion and his national record stood for decades after.

When Reilly asked him once where his talent emerged from, he replied with typical modesty: "I find talent is greatly overrated, Reilly. Starting out, I was no better or worse than the next person but I had one distinct advantage over most of my competitors".

"What was that?", asked Reilly, curious.

"The Woodlawn River."

"What are you talking about, Sean?"

"The Woodlawn River bordered the end of my father's farm, Mount Nirvana, and as a young lad I figured that, if I could only vault across that stream, I'd save myself a long walk by road to school.

"After many's the good wetting, I succeeded in crossing it. Each day, I'd take that short cut to and from school *via* that stream and, bit by bit, I got better and better at it.

"I must have crossed that stream 1,000 times a year over a 10-year period.

"I always credited my All Irelands to that Woodlawn River. It gave me what I suppose you could call purposeful practice."

Jim O'Connor came from the more urbane and salubrious surrounds of the Ennis Road in Limerick City, where his back garden sloped down to the expansive, wide and majestic River Shannon. There'd be no vaulting across it for a short cut to school.

Nonetheless, he too entertained dreams of winning an All Ireland someday at pole vaulting.

A gifted natural athlete, things were progressing swimmingly when he won the Leinster Championship in 1978, jumping one inch shy of 12 feet.

And then, he didn't win the All Ireland.

Reilly was gutted the night Jim arrived back from Belfield without a medal.

Jim was infinitely more sanguine.

"Reilly, the reality is you get three attempts in a pole vaulting competition. That amounts to about 21 seconds – between the run in and the jump – to strut your stuff.

"I've jumped 11' 11'' once before in a public competition and another handful of times on the top pitch training in Roscrea when nobody was looking.

"Today, I didn't do that – and somebody else did.

"I refuse to let 21 seconds of my life define who I am and how I feel. Now, let's park it and move on positively."

On 13 January last, 46 years after he didn't win the schools All Ireland, Jim O'Connor won the National Indoor Master Championship in pole vaulting in Athlone. His height of 2.8 metres now stands as the current national record.

In the pantheon of other illustrious Masters athletes, Eamon Coughlan appears on the spreadsheet at number 68. Jim is at 168.

"What inspired you, Jim?", asked Reilly, always on the sniff for an inspirational scoop.

"My damaged knee."

"What are you talking about, Jim?"

"I pulled ligaments in my knee and the medics suggested that strengthening my knee would help greatly.

"That became my goal. To strengthen my knees.

"I adapted my routines to get up at 5:55am each morning and be in the gym at 7am. Five mornings a week.

"And gradually, I began to look forward to the practice. The sense of space in being up and awake and alive when few others are. The cycle to the gym on both frosty mornings and sunny mornings. The camaraderie of chatting and having the *craic* with other like-minded gym members.

"I discovered that the benefits of regular practice in the gym were available to me 100% of the time, whereas the euphoria of winning a title is fleeting and transient.

"The practice – not the winning – that's why you stay in the game.

"And as my knees began to strengthen, and as my confidence and energy and self-esteem began to increase, I noticed a new voice in my head I named 'Maybe'.

"Maybe I could start pole vaulting again. Maybe I could get good at it. Maybe I could enter competitions again. Maybe I could win that medal I left behind 46 years ago.

"I credit my All Ireland to my damaged knee. It gave me what I suppose you could call purposeful practice."

Reilly wondered where he'd heard that before!

INSIGHTS

- In the most extensive study ever undertaken into the origins of success, the American psychologist Anders Ericsson studied the results of violinists at the renowned Music Academy of West Berlin in Germany. By the age of 20, the best violinists had practiced an average of 10,000 hours – more than 2,000 hours more than the good violinists and more than 6,000 hours longer than those aspiring to become music teachers.

- Ericsson's irrefutable conclusion was that practice, not talent, is the ultimate determinant of excellence. And he further found that there were no exceptions to the pattern: nobody had reached the elite group without copious amounts of practice, and nobody who worked their socks off failed to excel.

- Sean Murphy and Jim O'Connor call it 'purposeful practice'. Purposeful practice is the decisive factor distinguishing the best from the rest.

- The journey is as important as the destination. Enjoy the practice and let the score look after itself.

- Avoid letting 21-second outcomes define your entire life. It's amazing just how often we can allow one bad experience ruin our entire day.

- It's never too late to win an All Ireland.

QUESTION

- What's your Woodlawn River?

POSTSCRIPT

Dr. Sean Murphy passed on in 2021. There would be no Western Branch of the Roscrea Past Pupils' Union but for Sean. In fact, there might be no Roscrea College but for Sean. When the debate raged back in 2017 as to whether the College should close or remain open, Sean stood up.

He made an impassioned plea that the College must stay open in order to continue to give students from the surrounding locality the best chance at realising their potential.

That was quintessential Sean Murphy. When others were debating budgets and corporate governance and convoluted educational theories, Sean reverted to the students. He always put the person – be it student or patient – front and centre.

After 18 minutes in Donnybrook on Wednesday last, Roscrea trailed Newbridge by 22 points in the first round of the Leinster Senior Cup. Some fair-weather supporters had already begun their ignominious exit towards the Bective clubhouse.

Reilly had, as he sometimes does, a quiet word with Sean across the veil: "I wonder, Sean, should we have voted to close the College?"

When the final whistle blew, the scoreboard read Newbridge 22 – Roscrea 25.

It was Sean's way of reminding Reilly of the Woodlawn River.

43

WHAT'S IN A NAME?

What's in a name? That which we call a rose by any other name would smell just as sweet.

William Shakespeare, *Romeo & Juliet*

R eilly met him on his very first hour as a boarder in Roscrea.

Half a dozen heartbroken 12-year olds fell in forlornly and sheepishly on the cold tiles of the austere front hall of the College.

For most, they were experiencing the first serious separation from their mothers since the severing of their umbilical cords at birth.

And although they made unconvincing attempts at masking the terror, all wondered what the future would portend for them.

For some, the transition from home to boarding school life, would occur in a gradual and almost imperceptible manner.

For the tall, reserved, red-haired guy beside Reilly, it would be a complete and utter identity transformation.

A kindly Cistercian monk, An tAthair Éanna MacIonnraic, draped in black and white robes, happened to pass the group and instantly decked their despair. He caringly went around the group, asking the lads their names and where they'd come from.

For most, it was a reassuring reminder that, whilst An tAthair Éanna certainly wasn't their mother, there was a sense of safety and care and hope that things might work out.

For Reilly, it was a rare case of hitting the jackpot from the get-go.

When An tAthair Éanna discovered he came from close to *Conamara* and spoke reasonable Irish – two of the *grás* of his life after God – the stars aligned. For the following five years, he and Reilly would illegally share hundreds of cigarettes, discussing affairs of the world *as gaeilge*.

An tAthair's eyes lit up again when he cast his gaze on the tall, reserved, red-haired boy beside Reilly.

"You must be that boy's brother from Waterford who was with us 10 years ago!"

"No, Father. I'm from Rathkeale in County Limerick and I'm the eldest in my family."

"Well, in that case you're a dead-ringer for him. The height; the demeanour; the hair. Oh, I've a desperate head for names. What was his name at all?"

At precisely that moment, the President of the College, Fr. Peter Garvey, who had an encyclopaedic memory for faces and names passed by.

"What was the name of that boy from Waterford we had who looks just like this boy?"

"Paddy Lawless", says Fr. Peter, with absolute clarity and recall.

The former Neil Johnson never did get the opportunity to formally introduce himself.

From that moment on, until the day he departed the front gates of the College five years later after completing his Leaving Certificate, he was only ever known as Paddy Lawless.

His name notwithstanding, he very quickly became something of a legend.

Roscrea excelled in two disciplines – athletics and debating – and aspired to be great at rugby.

Paddy Lawless would quickly become an All Ireland Champion cross-country running champion and would later become a European award-winning public speaker.

With his speed, height and agility, he was a prolific try scorer. His scoring would most certainly have been even greater had Reilly outside him not knocked on the ball so often or thrown him so many forward passes.

Given his formative experience in Roscrea, it is perhaps little surprise that Paddy elected to study psychology in UCG.

As providence would have it, Reilly bumped into him again on their first day of Freshers' Week in Smokey Joe's cafeteria.

Paddy was enthusiastically chatting up the ravishing Riona Madden from Whitestrand, when Reilly cheerfully interrupted their *amorés*.

"Paddy Lawless, you were always quick on your feet, but you just can't rock in here from Rathkeale and rob us of our loveliest ladies", jested Reilly good-naturedly.

"Reilly, I want a word. Outside."

"What's your problem, Paddy? If you play your cards right, you could end up marrying that girl."

"Reilly, I want to make one message clear. For five years, I tolerated being called 'Paddy Lawless'. From today on, I begin a new identity. I am reverting to the name my parents chose for me. From this day on, my name is Neil. Neil Johnson. Understood?"

Reilly didn't need to be a student of psychology to understand implicitly.

Standing then at 6 foot 3 inches, and toned like a current Limerick hurler, Reilly understood.

As did each of the Roscrea lads in UCG, who also were firmly appraised of the change of name. By the time he graduated in 1983, everyone in Galway knew Paddy Lawless for who he really was: Neil Johnson.

Neil became a prominent member of the young Galway business community and became President of Junior Chamber Galway. In this role, he won the European Speaker of the Year in 1995 and was later made a Senator of the organisation in recognition of his impact.

Ray Rooney, the Galway-based businessperson, had conceived the idea of creating a centre for cardiac excellence in the West of Ireland. He was looking for a CEO to establish the organisation and drive it on.

Rooney's vision, combined with Johnson's executive acumen, would prove a Godsend for the people of the West of Ireland.

Neil knew at first hand the power and importance of a name and one of his primary victories was the creation of the name 'Croí'. Reilly acknowledged from the get-go that the name was pure marketing gold. It's memorable, pronounceable, suggestive of what it's about, totally unique, and An tAthair Éanna would have wholly approved.

From his early days in Roscrea, Neil had excelled as a communicator of clarity and excellence. He would now exploit this skill to explain to the people of Galway and the West the need for improved cardiac care and, more specifically, the investment.

Although Reilly is biased, Neil was the pioneer of professional fundraising in the West of Ireland. He brought it to an entirely different level.

Many will still remember the giant sculpture of a thermometer in the front of the Regional Hospital that displayed how much money Croí was seeking and how much it had currently raised.

This morning, in Galway and the West of Ireland, thousands of people will wake up – Reilly included – who mightn't have but for the purpose, leadership and acumen of Neil Johnson.

That's impact.

Last week, Reilly got a phone call from Don Colleran, the prominent Galway auctioneer, informing him that he needed to change Neil Johnson's title in his phone contacts.

"I did that 40 years ago, Don", says Reilly, smugly.

"You mustn't have heard, Reilly. Neil has been awarded a Doctor of Laws (LLD) by the University of Galway. From now on, we're expected to call him 'Dr. Johnson'."

INSIGHTS

- Names are important but it's what's beneath the bonnet that really counts.

- It wouldn't have mattered a *tráinín* whether Paddy Lawless had been called Neil Johnson or The Croí Guy, or Dr. Johnson or Jack Spratt – his character and actions and impact would have shone through irrespective.

- That's the thing about the great ones. They're not defined so much by their names, as by their character and actions and impact.

- Riona Madden continues to be as radiant as ever. The hundreds of Bish students she inspired over the years will testify to this. The thing is, they may know her better as Mrs. Johnson! But what's ever in a name?

- Your identity is important and the great news is that you can upgrade it like Neil anytime you intentionally choose.

- Always remember that your primary role as a business leader is to execute. That's what CEO stands for: Chief *Executive* Officer.

- Life isn't just about earning an income. That's important. But if you can earn an income helping other people, like Neil, then that's awesome.

QUESTIONS

- How powerful is your character?
- How powerful is your impact?
- How many people are feeling better today as a result of your influence?

44

THE ULTIMATE COMMITMENT

I'll go and do the best I can,
I'll do what must be done.
I'll go cause I'm a lifeboat man,
I am my father's son.

Jerry Earley & John Gallagher, *I'll Go*

The first thing Reilly noticed on alighting from the ferry on Arranmore Island was a massive monument dedicated to the men who rescued the S.S. *Stolwijk* in 1940.

"What's that all about, Joe?", he enquired off Joe Coyle.

Reilly and a tribe of SMACHT colleagues were visiting Donegal on a mission of drink and discovery and were being led by big Joe Coyle, a great disciple of SMACHT and a true son of Tír Conaill and the Bluestack Mountains.

"Get your ass on to this here bicycle, Reilly, and you'll learn what that monument can teach you about business and life later."

Reilly wasn't for arguing and for the next three hours he indulged in one of the most spectacular cycling trips of his life. It called on all their strength and fitness and endurance. Up steep mountains and across windswept valleys and out as far west as you can go – out to the very edge of the continent of Europe itself. Out to Arranmore lighthouse.

As always, things get intensified and polarised at the edges. The heights; the drops; the light; the darkness; the isolation; the intense presence of intimacy and belonging and being.

There were no lectures or workshops or Zoom calls at the lighthouse. The imagery spoke for itself. A beacon of light calling voyagers to an entire continent and warning them of the rocks and reefs that might threaten their journey.

Upon their return, Joe ushered them into Earley's Bar, where nibbles and libations were awaiting. And after four months of Covid-induced abstinence from draught porter, no pints ever tasted as sweet.

Following the meal, Joe introduced them to Jerry Earley – proprietor, lifeboat man and musician.

Reilly was seduced utterly by the Donegal accent. When hiring ace telesales personnel, he always hired people from Donegal. They outsold any other telesales people in the world by a factor of three to one. Maybe because it's constantly being buffeted and cleansed and bleached by the on-shore winds, but the Arranmore version of the Donegal accent is the purest of all.

When Jerry Earley began to recount to the group the events of the days of 5 and 6 December 1940, there wasn't a hair lying flat on Reilly's neck.

"At 10:30am on 5 December 1940, *Stolwijk*'s rudder broke off the coast of Donegal. Many attempts were made to repair it but they were futile, due to the weather. The anchor was dropped but the chain snapped and, even going in full reverse did not halt the ship's steady drift toward the rocky Irish coastline.

"The Arranmore lifeboat was notified late in the evening of 6 December 1940 of the ship in distress and given an approximate location.

"Eight Arranmore lifeboat people were called that evening and asked would they mount a sortie to rescue the stricken boat in what was effectively a suicide mission, given the conditions.

"Everyone of the eight said, 'I'll go'.

"The lifeboat reached *Stolwijk* at noon in very stormy conditions.

"The lifeboat anchored to windward and drifted close to the boat and then fired a line to the crew so a breeches buoy could be used to transfer the men. This procedure was repeated three times as the line kept breaking. It took four hours for all 18 survivors to be rescued in this way, each spending upwards of five minutes in the water.

"It took the lifeboat a further five hours to reach Burtonport on the mainland, during which she was nearly swamped by heavy seas.

"I'm a native of Arranmore and was aware of the rescue from a young age and, although most of the crew were still alive during my childhood, the men involved rarely, if ever, spoke about that night. It was not their way to seek praise or indulge in self-congratulation.

"75 years after that famous rescue, myself and my cousin, John Gallagher, were somehow called to write a song about it.

"It's called *I'll Go*."

And as Jerry tuned his guitar, and began singing his song[1] in his own pub, on his own island, Reilly understood what it meant to be called.

INSIGHTS

- Every minute, of every hour, of every day, you are being called:
  - Called to get up when the alarm clock rings and you'd rather snooze and snuggle back to bed.
  - Called to put a smile on your puss, when all you want is to pucker and pout.

---

[1]   Listen to Jerry sign the song on YouTube here *https://youtu.be/WmG_jrBcgYM*. As far as I know, it is the most requested song ever on Highland Radio.

- o Called to make hard decisions you'd rather avoid or leave to someone else.
- o Called to risk failure and loss of face, when it would be easier to do nothing.
- o Called to console and understand and love, when it would be easier to be consoled and understood and loved.
- o Called to give, when it would be easier to receive.
- Like those eight heroes on Arranmore, you too are being quietly called on your own heroic journey. Every one of us is. For some, it's to start a new business. For others it's to leave a partner or a career that's stagnated or atrophied. For others again, it's to confront the journey of a serious illness and all that it will entail.
- The thing is: when you're called, like the men of Arranmore, will you go?

QUESTIONS

- What is your deepest calling?
- Will you go when you're called?

TIME

45

BARBER'S BLOCK

I only ever write when I am inspired.
Fortunately, that's at 9am every morning.

William Somerset Maugham

Mattie, Reilly's barber, upbraided him jovially on his failure to post a blog the previous Sunday. Although issued in jest, the comment stung Reilly. He wasn't letting Mattie away with it.

"Mattie, you need to be inspired to be able to write. You just can't come up with a blog out of the ether."

"Just as well there's no such thing as barber's block then, Reilly!"

"What are you talking about, Mattie?"

"Barber's block. Whether I feel like cutting hair or not, I show up here every morning at 9am and cut hair just like it says I do on the door. Us barbers have no regard for what you writers call 'writer's block'."

As Kenny Rogers might put it, Reilly "found an ace that I could keep".

INSIGHTS

- Pros show up whether they feel like it or not.

- Pros don't wait to be inspired to take action. They understand that, in the game of life, action always precedes accomplishment. They get that when you show up, the Muse does also. She always eludes those who hopelessly wait in vain for her.

- Pros keep their word every time. They value commitment above involvement; agreements over expectations. They do what they say they do; as a consequence, pros are judicious in the extreme about making commitments with others.

- Pros avoid trading in expectations. They make agreements – and keep them.

- Amateurs believe in writer's block. Their excuses are bigger than their goals. They live their lives waiting to be inspired. Stop making excuses.

QUESTIONS

- In what areas in your business and life have you been experiencing and tolerating writer's block?

- What agreements have you that you absolutely keep?

- What agreements have you been reneging on recently?

- Who have you in your accountability circle to call you out when you renege on your commitments? Get more of them on the bus.

46

HOW THOMAS EDISON
MANAGED TIME

Dost thou love life? Then do not squander time,
for that's the stuff life is made of.

Benjamin Franklin

Not many people know this but Reilly's great-grandfather worked with the inventor, Thomas Edison, in his laboratory in Menlo Park, New Jersey.

The two men shared a common love of fishing and it was well-known that Edison used to spend at least an hour a day out fishing on the local lake.

However, the world's greatest inventor – the man who invented the phonograph, the motion picture camera and the electric light bulb – was a notoriously poor fisherman.

One day, Reilly's great-grandfather broached the subject with the great man: "Tommy, pardon me for saying this, but in all the years I've watched you fishing, I've never yet seen you hook a fish. For such a brilliant inventor, how come you're such a pathetic fisherman?"

"You're right, Reilly," said Edison. "I rarely ever catch a fish – for the simple reason that I never use a bait."

Reilly's great-grandfather thought this was incredulous.

"Why in the name of God would anyone go fishing without a bait?"

"Because when you fish without a bait, people don't bother you, and neither do the fish. It affords me the space to be still and to think and to be."

The mysticism was lost on Reilly's great-grandfather..

"Is this being still and thinking and being not just a waste of time when you could be working hard inside in the laboratory?"

"Reilly, my brightest scientists struggled unsuccessfully for months to design a filament that would light a bulb. After almost 1,000 failed experiments, they told me it was impossible. And last Monday, while out here fishing without a bait, I discovered the solution myself. It was there all the time, sitting in the palm of my hands."

"What are you taking about, Tommy?"

"Bamboo, Reilly. As I sat there fishing with my bamboo rod, without a bait, it occurred to me to try bamboo as the filament for the light bulb."

And the rest, as they say, is history.

INSIGHTS

- Make regular time periods in your life to go fishing without a bait.
- To be still; and to think; and to be.

- And let the omnipotent universal intelligence work its magic within you.

QUESTIONS

- How much time will you allocate to being still and thinking and being this week?
- Will you time activate it in your diary now? It's as important as any other appointment you have this week!

47

FINISH WHAT YOU START

Don't Quit

When things go wrong, as they sometimes will, and the road you're trudging seems all uphill,
When the funds are low and the debts are high, and you want to smile, but you have to sigh,
When care is pressing you down a bit, rest if you must, but don't you quit.
Life is queer with its twists and turns, as every one of us sometimes learns.
And many a failure turns about when he might have won had he stuck it out.
Don't give up though the pace seems slow; you may succeed with another blow.
Often the goal is nearer than it seems to a faint and faltering man.
Often the struggler has given up when he might have captured the victor's cup,
And he learned too late when the night slipped down, how close he was to the golden crown.
Success is failure turned inside out, the silver tint of the clouds of doubt,
And you never can tell how close you are. It may be near when it seems afar.
So stick to the fight when you're hardest hit. It's when things seem worst that you mustn't quit.

Edgar Guest

When Reilly gets tired and feels like giving up he never fails to get uplifted and inspired by the John Stephen Akhwari story.

TV producer Bud Greenman was packing away his gear following the 1968 Mexico City Marathon. It had been over an hour since he had televised the iconic Ethiopian runner, Mamo Wolde, as he cruised, almost effortlessly, across the finish line in a time of 2:20:26.

Just then his production assistant came running up, yelling: "Hey, Mr. Greenman. There's one left. You ought to film him".

And sure enough, into the darkened and almost deserted stadium hobbled a heavily-bandaged and clearly-injured competitor. Each step caused him to wince painfully.

John Stephen Akhwari, the Tanzanian competitor, had fallen badly in the 11th mile while jockeying for position. In the fall, he dislocated his knee and badly damaged his shoulder as it was rammed against the pavement.

The few remaining spectators inside the stadium began to cheer and clap as Akhwari struggled to reach the finish line. As he crossed it, he fell for the second time, clutching his knee in agony.

The crowd roared their acclaim.

Greenman had recorded every scintilla of that excruciatingly painful, courageous and emotional finish. In addition, he got to interview Akhwari immediately afterwards and began by enquiring about the runner's injuries and the pain and the trauma.

He then asked what Reilly thought was a great question: "Mr. Akhwari, why did you bother finishing the race, given your injuries and knowing full well you had no chance of winning?"

Akhwari seemed baffled by the question.

"Mr. Greenspan, I don't think you understand. My country did not send me 5,000 miles to start the race. They sent me to finish it!"

Akhwari was the last to finish – in 54th place.

Interestingly, 75 started the race.

INSIGHTS

- Finishing is much more difficult than starting. Day 1 is infinitely sexier than Day 2 – or certainly, Day 336. There's a reason your gym is much emptier in December than it is in January. If you're struggling to finish, think of John Stephen Akhwari.

- And despite the populist rhetoric, winning is not nearly as important as it's cracked up to be by society. Long after the disappointment of defeat has dissipated, what will remain for those who participated will be the insatiable thrill of competing. This was what Pierre de Coubertin had in mind when founding the modern Olympic Games.
- The ultimate victories are those private victories with ourselves, where we take ourselves on and finish what we start.
- In the final analysis, it's the finishers who are the winners.

QUESTION

- What are those things that you started this year that you get to finish, irrespective of how difficult it feels or how far behind you are?

48

LESS IS MORE

Simplicity is the ultimate sophistication.

Leonardo da Vinci

Everyone sniggered when Reilly's buddy, Flaherty, signed up for a course in the university on of all things – Philosophy.

And they laughed openly when they heard of his performance in the exam at the conclusion of the first semester.

The Professor, an academic snob of gargantuan proportion, stormed into the examination hall – UCG's hallowed *Aula Maxima* – and dramatically hurled a chair onto the stage.

"Prove to me that this chair doesn't exist", he bellowed to the class. "No questions permitted. But take all the time you require. There is no time limit."

There was much amusement when Flaherty departed the hall for the College Bar within the first minute.

Many of the more erudite, learned and dedicated students embraced the opportunity of unlimited time and wrote for hours on end. It was said that veritable theses were written that day on the existence, or not, of that chair on the sterile boards of the *Aula*.

But there was absolute consternation a month later when the results were posted on the official notice board in the University's quadrangle.

Out of a cohort of the good and great of Galway's intelligentsia, Flaherty topped the class with a first class honours result.

The College Bar was a hotbed of intrigue that day.

Flaherty appeared, just like the boy Jesus in the Temple, 2,000 years earlier, surrounded by the wise people of the time.

"Flaherty", they beseeched in awe and disbelief. "What did you write in your examination paper on why the chair didn't exist?"

"What chair?", said Flaherty innocently.

INSIGHTS

- Sometimes, less *IS* more.

QUESTION

- What areas of your business and life could you simplify?

49

IF YOU SNOOZE, YOU LOSE

If you want to change your life and maybe the world, start off by making your bed.

Admiral William H. McRaven, *Make Your Bed*

Early is on time, on time is late, and late is unacceptable.

Eric Jerome Dickey, *Sleeping with Strangers*

Success is nothing more than a few simple disciplines, practiced every day; while failure is simply a few errors in judgment, repeated every day. It is the accumulative weight of our disciplines and our judgments that leads us to either fortune or failure.

Jim Rohn

Reilly's first error of judgement of the new school year was to arrive up late to the dormitory on the first night back after the summer holidays. He'd been out in the saloon, smoking with the hard men, and had utterly lost track of the time.

By the time he did get there, every other bed had been taken, except for the second last bed in the innermost corner of the dormitory. As he placed his suitcase onto the bare and hard mattress, one of the lads pointed to the bed beside him and said: "I hope we get a good prefect, Reilly, 'cause like it, or like it not, you're next to him for the rest of the year".

With that, the door burst open and Springer took ownership of the room by striding the length of the dormitory and proceeding to hurl his bags forcibly onto the bed beside Reilly.

Turning to the dormitory, he waited for complete silence before addressing them: "Now guys, it's like this. I have high and demanding expectations for myself for this year. All of them require a good night's sleep and an orderly and well-behaved dormitory. I'll expect full compliance with the following three ground rules:

- Lights out and complete silence by 10.30pm.
- Hit those boards before the 7am bell stops ringing.
- Make your bed before you do anything else each morning.

Any questions?"

Reilly committed his second error in quick succession.

"Springer, that's not fair. We never had to do that with our prefect last year".

"You're spot on, Reilly. Life isn't fair but the moment you learn that, strangely life gets better. Now Reilly, any more lessons you'd like to learn this evening?"

Reilly thought better of it and went off to sleep dreaming of a cute little girl from Donegal he'd met that summer. He was still dreaming about her when the bell rang. And when the bell stopped. It was his third error of judgement.

He marvelled at Springer's strength. Like a JCB hoisting a pallet of bricks off a slab, he effortlessly shovelled Reilly up in his arms, mattress and all, and asked the entire dormitory to observe the law of gravity in practice. Raising Reilly and the mattress up to chest level, he opened his arms and let gravity reacquaint Reilly with the hard bed.

It was the last time that year that anyone in the third year dormitory either slept past the bell or failed to make their bed.

Later that year, Springer would go on to captain the Leinster Schoolboys rugby side and subsequently become captain of the Irish Schoolboys side. Despite his sporting commitments, he would also do an outstanding Leaving Cert. A bare three years later, he would win his first cap as a fully-fledged international on the Irish senior team.

As for Reilly, he learned on that seminal morning that getting out of bed is never easy. But it's the same level of difficulty getting out when the bell rings as pressing the snooze button and being behind for the rest of the day.

He also learned that no matter how bad a day you had, you at least always had the satisfaction of returning to a made bed.

INSIGHTS

- As a general principle, arriving late immediately puts you on the hind foot and under pressure. Develop the discipline and habit of always being on time.

- Springer was not just a good prefect. He was a great prefect. Through his example, Reilly learned the power of discipline and routine and habit.

- More significantly, Reilly learned the importance of a victory with yourself first thing in the morning. He learned that how you show up first thing in the morning determines greatly how you show up for the rest of the day. If you begin the day by choosing to press the snooze button, it'll likely set you up for a day of further procrastination and dodging the realities of life.

- Have clear and high expectations for yourself, your business and your family. In general, high expectations improve performance, whereas low expectations seem to undermine achievement.

- Ground rules are critically important. Imagine a game without rules!

QUESTIONS

- What difference would it make if you got up each morning when the alarm rings?
- What difference would it make if you made your bed first thing each morning?
- What difference would it make if you had a 'Springer' on your side?
- What difference would it make if you had a positive expectation for yourself, your family and your business?
- What difference would it make if you had ground rules for your business?

POSTSCRIPT

Reilly recalls attending a rugby international in Landsdowne Road in the mid-'80s. Back in those days, the substitutes and alickadoos used sit in a cordoned-off section in the lower stand. As Reilly was going to his seat, Springer, who was a sub that day, recognised him and proceeded to roar at him in front of everyone: "Reilly, did you make your bed this morning?"

50

THE TAPE OF LIFE

*Things which matter most must never be at the mercy of
things which matter least.*

Goethe

D id you ever wonder why things seem inexorably to go wrong always on a Friday evening, just when there's no help available? The baby spikes a temperature. The dog devours every last one of the mother-in-law's sleeping tablets. The dodgy tooth flares up into what you know is a certain abscess. The Internet goes down, just as the match kicks off.

Reilly had started tucking in to one of Sitar's tandoori chicken specials and a few pints of his favourite IPA before the All Blacks *v* Argentina game.

Just then, water began dribbling ominously down the side of the wall from beneath the immersion heater upstairs. Reilly chose optimistically to turn his back to it in the hope that it might miraculously stop.

But not Mrs. Reilly, who believes that problems should be confronted early and often.

"Get Nicky Hanley in here fast before he goes off fishing for the weekend or else we'll be as flooded by Monday morning", commanded Mrs. Reilly with scant regard for either Reilly's rest or relaxation.

Reilly knew from past experience that there'd be no let-up until this problem was rectified. So he dutifully tracked Nicky down to the only place he would be on a Friday evening: Cooke's Thatched Bar on Cooke's Corner.

It was no hardship. Reilly and Nicky fell instantly into discussing their common area of expertise – that year's fishing, and the proceeding 60 years, on the Corrib. So it was a good hour later before Reilly remembered the purpose of his visit.

"Nicky, I need you to fix a leak in the immersion *toot sweet*, as they say in France."

"I'm sorry, Reilly. I'm going fishing, as they say in Henry Street."

Now Reilly and Nicky had history. Their fathers had fished together. Their kids had gone to school together. Nicky grudgingly acceded that Reilly was a 'middling' angler. Reilly acknowledged that Nicky was the best plumber in the west of Ireland. If Nicky would oblige anyone, it would be Reilly. And, if anyone could persuade Nicky, it would be Reilly.

"I'll make it worth your while, Nicky."

"I'm going fishing, Reilly."

Reilly knew he was in the mother of an arm-wrestle and would need to summon all of his silken negotiation skills.

"Nicky, do you remember the year Uncle Stiofáin and myself won the *Bráithereacht*?" (the oldest and most prestigious angling competition on the lower lake).

Reilly could see he'd connected and jabbed quickly again.

"Do you recall the eight fine trout we landed that day and the lake as flat as a princess' looking-glass?"

Reilly knew from the look on Nicky's face that he'd landed another body-blow.

"After the weigh-in, everyone was asking us what we caught the trout on but Stiofáin had sworn me to secrecy. Nobody, outside of myself and Stiofáin, has ever seen that *brickeen* lure, Nicky. I'm prepared to give it to you, if you'll fix the leak."

Nicky paused for an eternity. Reilly sensed capitulation and impending victory. He resolved to remain humble.

"Reilly, what part of 'I'm going fishing' do you not understand?"

"Ah, I understand it implicitly, Nicky, just as long as you fix the leak."

Nicky proceeded to slowly extricate a measuring tape from his inside pocket.

"Do you know what this is, Reilly?"

"Sure I do, Nicky. It's a measuring tape. It must be the ultimate ubiquitous tool in your trade."

"Cushty, Reilly, as Del Boy would say."

Pointing to a number at the top of the tape, Nicky asks Reilly: "What number is that?"

"70", says Reilly, who always fancied himself on numbers.

"And what number is that down there?"

"57", says Reilly.

"Precisely", says Nicky. "Now, Reilly, watch my lips.

"At 70, my father was carried out of that house across the road in a box. I'm now 57. And tomorrow morning, Reilly, I'm going fishing."

INSIGHTS

- Confront problems early and often.
- Hope is rarely a good strategy.
- Your time is finite. The demands on your time are infinite. The good news is that, like Nicky, you have choices.

- Some people have figured out what's important in their lives and have determined to see that through irrespectively. Others have identified what is important to them but end up succumbing to the priorities of others. Most however, have never seriously asked themselves the question.

QUESTIONS

- Have you identified what's most important in your business and life?
- Are you fulfilling YOUR priorities, or other people's?
- When was the last time you said "No" like Nicky?
- What would you do today if you were at 70 on Nicky's 'tape of life'?

51

IT'S A SMALL WORLD

Someday, your network will equal your net worth.

Tim Saunders

Reilly will never forget his first trip to America. It was the summer of 1986 and he'd never been more excited about anything in his life. He'd discovered that his friend, Mártan Ó Ciardha, who was Head of Sport for Raidio na Gaeltachta, was tasked with live-broadcasting the world title fight between Barry McGuigan and Steve Cruz in Caesar's Palace Hotel in Las Vegas.

As an absolute sports fanatic, nothing would do Reilly but to go along with Mártan and, after much perseverance, Mártan finally acquiesced. Reilly would later appear on the credits as Production Assistant for the show, which was really just a benign euphemism for messenger boy.

They departed Shannon on the morning of 21 June and Reilly was beside himself with excitement and anticipation.

As per instructions, they hired a car at the airport to take them and their equipment to Caesar's Palace Hotel.

As Reilly had never been outside of Ireland before, it took him a while to adjust to the different driving regulations. As navigator, he was quick to observe that the cars appeared to drive on the right-hand side of the road as opposed to *Conamara*, where many drive on the left.

As they approached the city centre through the Red Light district, Reilly's eyes were on sticks. One after another, he began pointing out the various clubs to Mártan and it was probably this *divarsion* that temporarily distracted him.

He failed to notice, until it was too late, that the traffic lights had turned to red and there was a large car stopped at the lights which unfortunately they crashed into.

As with most rear-end collisions, it's generally worse on the vehicle in front. To be honest, apart from being a tad shaken, Reilly and Mártan were fine.

That was until the door opened and a man, clearly of Italian extraction, alighted from the vehicle in front.

Reilly knew immediately that their goose was cooked. He'd seen *The Godfather* a dozen times in the Claddagh Palace and he knew there could only be one outcome.

And there would have been too, except that at that precise moment, a police motorcycle screeched to a halt beside them.

Reilly assimilated it all in jig time. If the guy in the car looked like an actor from *The Godfather*, the cop was a ringer for Ponch's partner in the

TV show *Chips*. He had the same swagger, blond hair, blue eyes, and a massive revolver tucked into his trousers.

He first restrained the Italian and then proceeded to take a detailed statement.

He then took at least a further three statements from some of the bystanders who'd witnessed the accident.

This afforded Mártan an invaluable opportunity to compose himself and prepare his own presentation. When you present a live daily programme on national radio, you're used to performing under pressure.

"Name", says the cop, without any introduction or small talk whatsoever.

Mártan was unfazed.

"Guard, you won't believe it, but we're not from America at all. We've just arrived in on the plane from Ireland for the fight between wee Barry and Cruz."

Mártan's words fell like lead balloons.

"Now let me make myself abundantly clear", says the policeman, authoritatively. "It appears you've committed a serious accident. I've any amount of witnesses prepared to testify that you rear-ended an innocent and law-abiding citizen. Now, I'm asking you for the last time, what's your name?"

Mártan knew the game was up and resolved to comply obediently. In his most mellifluous *Conamara* brogue, he says: "Guard, my name is Mártan Ó Ciardha".

It was clear that Blondie was having difficulty with the Irish. Sometimes, even Reilly himself, who was a fluent speaker, had difficulty picking up everything Mártan would say.

"Where ya from, Keera?"

Mártan was about to say he wasn't from America at all, but thought better of it, and resolved to tell the whole truth and nothing but the truth.

"Guard, I come from a small place called Baile an Domhnalláin."

"Where's that?", says the cop, furiously trying to write the location down.

"It's about two miles from An Spidéil", says Mártan truthfully.

"And where's this place called Spidale?", says the cop impatiently.

"It's about 12 miles from the town of Galway."

This time, the cop succeeded in spelling the word.

"And where's this place called Galway?"

"It's about 133 miles from Dublin, the capital of all Ireland", says Mártan, happy to drag the conversation out to what seemed its inevitable conclusion.

The cop proceeded to write a number of explanatory notes before pushing his head squarely inside the window of the lads' car and asking quietly: "What speed was Luigi reversing at when he hit ye?"

It transpired that the cop had the same surname as Mártan and both his parents came from the *Conamara* Gaeltacht.

Isn't it a small world!

INSIGHTS

- Even when situations appear to be impossible, always believe that there's a way out.
- The old adage still holds that 'It's not always *what* you know, but *who* you know, that's most important.'
- Ask 'who' before 'how'.
- Always be proud of where you come from. It's part of your identity.

QUESTION

- Who is in your network?

52

THE ULTIMATE TIME MANAGEMENT TOOL

Live life closer to the edge. Things go faster there.
The victories. The learnings. The discoveries.
Pádraig Ó Céidigh

The past is just a mirage. A soft illusion into which we
escape, in order to avoid the present.
Brian Friel

When he's fishing, he's fishing. When he's drinking, he's
drinking. When he's working, he's working.
Cháv Dever, *The Ultimate Time Manager*

Reilly spent most of the week on edge. With customers; staff members; bank managers; projects; even family. By Saturday, his head was so fried he knew he needed some space.

He headed West. West to Inis Oirr. The smallest of the Aran Islands. Nine miles off the Clare coast. The most Westerly point in Europe.

Even getting there was not without its frustrations. He got lampooned behind a big German touring bus outside of Ballyvaughan. Its average cruising speed was 20 mph and, even then, it would shudder to a complete halt at the onset of anything bigger than a bicycle.

Reilly was going ballistic.

He eventually succeeded in overtaking the bus on the second twist of the Corkscrew Hill. As the driver beeped furiously at him, Reilly waved back triumphantly.

He blazed into Doolin just in time to see them hauling the gangway on board the 11am ferry. He used every negotiating trick in the book with that ferryman to get on the boat. The ferryman wasn't buying any of them.

And by the time he finally reached Inis Oirr on the 12 noon ferry, all the bikes in the bicycle shop had been rented. That is, with the exception of one sad and dilapidated ladies' vehicle that had seen better times.

"*Bainfadh tú deatach as an* beauty *seo agus tá an clog ag obair ar fheabhas*" (You'll knock smoke out of this beauty and the bell is working perfectly), said Neassán, the handsome and roguish manager.

And Reilly did too. He took the entire week's frustration out on that bike. He hared back through Baile an tSéipéil and Baile an Chaisleáin, past Teampall Chaomhán and out to Gob na Cora, where the wreck of the *Plassey*, immortalised in the opening scene of the TV series, Father Ted, lies. And all the while he rang that bell, frantically scattering slews of terrified tourists to either side.

The vigorous exercise had blunted his anxiety but he was still tangibly on edge. He retraced his route with increased velocity and headed West. He kept going. Back past the beach and up by Baile Thiar and out past An Mionnnán. Even when the tarred road gave way to a stony *bóirín* with a grass verge up the middle, he pushed man and bike for all they were worth.

The bike surrendered first. He bounced the tyre off a jagged-edged stone and the tyre deflated instantly. Impetuously, he rang Neassán to solicit a lift back to civilisation but there was no signal on his phone. In fact, there was no wifi service whatsoever.

"What an apt metaphor for my life!", Reilly thought. "Broken down, lost and on the edge."

He heard her before he saw her.

"Aw shucks, not to worry. Better luck next time. Maybe you'll see it."

She was clearly American. There was no denying the accent. Or the sallow skin. Or the chestnut-coloured eyes. You only ever get that complexion in America..

"I beg your pardon", Reilly replied.

"The eel. You must have come to see the eel. You want to be healed. You couldn't have found Tobar Éanna by accident because it's not signposted."

Gesturing to a tiny field that she'd just emerged from, she explained: "It's the Holy Well of St. Enda, the patron saint of Aran, and it has never run dry in living memory. Legend has it that if you walk around the well seven times, reciting the Rosary, and look into the well and see an eel, that you'll be cured of whatever ails you."

"And have you seen the eel?", blurted Reilly, disbelievingly.

"I spent a week on the island as a student 25 years ago and visited this well every day. I'd heard that Brendan Behan had done it years before. Every day, for three whole months, he had escaped the contagion of chaos in his life and would visit here, and just be. He claimed later that it had been the most peaceful and tranquil and creative period of his entire life.

"The 'eel' I did encounter that week, however, was a magical Irishman in Tigh Ned's whom I fell impossibly in love with. He won my heart but then things happened and he slipped through my fingers. Like the elusive eel in the well.

"Love can be like that, don't you think? Mysterious. Miraculous. Magical. Elusive. If you're not mindful!

"This well, and how it makes me feel, has never left me. I take it with me wherever I go. I vowed that one day I'd return here with my daughter to check if the past was real, or simply a mirage."

After she'd left, Reilly skirted the stile and approached the well tentatively. He could have spared himself the melodrama because all that was there was a small well, flanked by a series of humble limestone flags.

He plonked himself down beside it and, for the first time that week, he surrendered. He surrendered utterly to the present moment.

And sometime later, he couldn't tell you how long, the eel appeared. In fact, it had been there all along. He had simply been mindless to it. He'd been too busy.

It lay draped on a bed of white daisies and yellow buttercups and orangey-red montbretia all over the field. It gurgled in the waters of the well that had been released from the darkness into the light. It coated his lips with sea-salt that was invigorating and tangy and cleansing to taste.

And it connected deeply and directly with him, through some Divine wifi. Through the spirits of Naomh Éanna and Behan and Synge who, before him, had all created so prolifically here. It was here that they were salved of their cares by the ultimate life management tool.

The Present Moment.

Back in Tigh Ned's, he caught her eye across the crowded bar. Beside her sat a stunning girl in her mid-20s with luscious tresses of auburn-red hair and the greenest eyes you ever saw. You only ever get that complexion in Ireland.

"Did you see it? Did you see the 'eel'?", she gesticulated to him with dramatic emphasis.

He nodded his head.

She smiled back knowingly.

INSIGHTS

- Make time to be on your own; and be silent; and still; and simply be.
- Find a Sacred Space – your own well – that you can escape to. Then imprint it on your mind, so you can take it with you anywhere and anytime, even in the loudest and busiest of places.
- Believe in a Higher Power that is accessible to you every second of every minute of every day. It is forever by your side.
- When love shows up, seize it with all you've got. Never let life get in the way of love.
- Live life closer to the edge. The Present Moment. It's the ultimate time management tool.

QUESTION

- Where is your Sacred Well?

SMACHT-LORE

In March 2019, Pádraic Ó Máille's business clients hit a serious challenge to their business: the Covid-19 pandemic.

Pádraic assumed it would last for a month or two and decided to keep his clients uplifted with a weekly story that was designed to be funny, uplifting and a touch provocative.

In order to help him achieve this, he hit on a character called 'Reilly', who would be part professor, part business guru, and mostly, a rogue.

The Life O'Reilly became a weekly source of wisdom, insight and levity for many hundreds of business people.

When word emerged that it might form the basis of a book, Reilly was accosted by a member of the publishing fraternity – an Irish Lobster – who informed him that many of his stories were not original.

Reilly was flattered.

That's the thing about great stories. They've been around the houses many times and continue to be welcome wherever they go.

Reilly undeniably concedes that almost all the stories in this book have been inspired by other people and circumstances.

Here is an attempt to credit some of the sources. Sincere apologies to those he may have omitted.

1. *Dedication*. Even the *Dedication* has been inspired by other writers – specifically, Jimmy Barnes, whose wonderful dedication appears in a book called *Working Class Man*.

2. *Introduction: Hide the Pill in the Peanut Butter*. Reilly first read a version of this story in a book called *Never Be Boring Again* by Doug Stevenson. He later heard Doug recite it in a hilarious YouTube clip called *The Science of the Art of Storytelling in Business*. Doug is one of the great pioneers and practitioners of storytelling in business.

3. *"Oh, My Darling Nora"*. Although the story is Reilly's, it was inspired by Dr. Paddy Gargan, a good friend of Reilly's, who actually was Jack Charlton's ghillie for a number of days back in those halcyon days of Irish soccer. Reilly's Uncle Stiofáin was a formative influence on the young Reilly and appears in many of these stories.

4. *A Paradigm Shift*. Reilly heard the late Stephen Covey tell his version of this story at a session in Trinity College, back in the 1990s.

5. *Find Your Lighthouse* was informed by a lovely article in *Forbes* called *Are You a Lighthouse Leader?* by Rodger Dean Duncan.

6. *How the Japs Bombed Bell Harbour*. There are many versions of this story told in the Burren in North Clare. In one, a farmer returns to his home after a long day on the farm and when his wife said to him "The Japs bombed Bell Harbour", his response was "Dheara, Mary dear, why would the Japs bomb Bell Harbour? Now, let's be having the tea".

7. As noted earlier, Professor Jim Ward and Dr. Aidan Daly, apart from being pioneering marketing academics and practitioners, were first and foremost servants to their students. Everything they aspired to had their students front and centre. Nothing pleased them more than to see their students succeed and they'd move mountains to ensure that happened.

8. *Just Checking*. Reilly heard Murray Raphel, author of *Up the Loyalty Ladder* tell this story at a seminar in Dublin in the 1990s. Murray is one of the great writers on retail marketing.

9. *Who's in Your Room?* was inspired by a great book called Who's in Your Room: The Secret to Creating Your Best Life, published in 2018 by Ivan Misner, Stewart Emery and Rick Sapio.

10. *The Ultimate Worry Formula* was inspired by Dale Carnegie's book *How to Stop Worrying and Start Living*. Written in 1948, it remains an enduring personal development classic.

11. *Stop Thinking like an Accountant* was informed by Mike Michalowicz's book *Profit First*.

Whilst you'll recognise many of the stories from other high profile speakers and writers, the majority were inspired by the members of SMACHT who trade their stories with each other on a weekly basis. Many thanks for allowing me into your confidence and allowing me to share your stories and insights and questions with a wider world.

Reilly is a needy character and, like Mark Twain, could "live for three whole months on one compliment". He'd sincerely like to thank all those readers of *The Life O'Reilly* who'd connect with him and give him regular feedback. Rarely would a Sunday morning elapse before there'd be a message from Kevin Dever or Jim Keating. That was massively appreciated during those dark days of Covid.

Pádraic would like to thank Brian O'Kane of Oak Tree Press. Brian's organisational skills ensured the book was published in a seriously speedy time frame. In addition, the experience was memorable, enjoyable and productive.

And finally, to you the readers of this book. If you enjoyed it, please recommend it to a friend or colleague. As someone once said, "It's not the author who makes a great book, it's the readers".

ABOUT THE AUTHOR

Pádraic Ó Máille, founder of SMACHT, has provided hundreds of business people with a safe, positive and proactive space to start, grow and, in many cases, sell their businesses.

SMACHT is virtually your own personal Board of Advisors where you meet to gain clarity, wisdom and accountability.

He is also an inspiring motivational speaker, who will get you thinking more clearly, dynamically and proactively. His themes are strategy; marketing; attitude; cash; human relations; and time management.

Pádraic is the author of *The Midas Power, Rocking Horse Shit*, and *The 3-Day Weekend*. His blog, *The Life O'Reilly*, helped sustain a positive attitude for hundreds of readers during Covid and continues to do so.

He lives with his wife Annie in the Burren, Co. Clare, Ireland and gets to swim in the Atlantic most days.

To discuss how he might inspire you or your team, contact him on p@omaille.ie or to subscribe to his free weekly blog, *The Life O'Reilly*, please go to www.omaille.ie.

OAK TREE PRESS

Oak Tree Press is Ireland's leading business book publisher, with an unrivalled reputation for quality titles across business, management, HR, law, marketing, and enterprise topics. Its publications are targeted at busy entrepreneurs and managers – always focussing on the effective communication of business information.

OAK TREE PRESS

NSC Campus, Mahon, Cork T12 XY2N
T: + 353 021 230 7021
E: info@oaktreepress.com
W: www.oaktreepress.com / www.SuccessStore.com